United States
Department
of Agriculture

Forest Service

Rocky Mountain
Research Station

General Technical Report
RMRS-GTR-253

March 2011

USDA

How to Generate and Interpret Fire Characteristics Charts for Surface and Crown Fire Behavior

Patricia L. Andrews, Faith Ann Heinsch, and Luke Schelvan

Andrews, Patricia L.; Heinsch, Faith Ann; Schelvan, Luke. 2011. **How to generate and interpret fire characteristics charts for surface and crown fire behavior.** Gen. Tech. Rep. RMRS-GTR-253. Fort Collins, CO: U.S. Department of Agriculture, Forest Service, Rocky Mountain Research Station. 40 p.

Abstract

A fire characteristics chart is a graph that presents primary related fire behavior characteristics—rate of spread, flame length, fireline intensity, and heat per unit area. It helps communicate and interpret modeled or observed fire behavior. The Fire Characteristics Chart computer program plots either observed fire behavior or values that have been calculated by another computer program such as the BehavePlus fire modeling system. Program operation is described in this report, and its flexibility in format, color, and labeling is demonstrated for use in a variety of reports. A chart produced by the program is suitable for inclusion in briefings, reports, and presentations. Example applications are given for fire model understanding, observed crown fire behavior, ignition pattern effect on fire behavior, prescribed fire planning, briefings, and case studies. The mathematical foundation for the charts is also described. Separate charts are available for surface fire and crown fire because of differences in the flame length model used for each.

Keywords: wildland fire, fire behavior, fire modeling, fire spread, fire intensity, computer program

You may order additional copies of this publication by sending your mailing information in label form through one of the following media. Please specify the publication title and number.

Publishing Services

Telephone	(970) 498-1392
FAX	(970) 498-1122
E-mail	rschneider@fs.fed.us
Web site	http://www.fs.fed.us/rmrs
Mailing Address	Publications Distribution
	Rocky Mountain Research Station
	240 West Prospect Road
	Fort Collins, CO 80526

Cover Photos: *Surface fire, Wayne Cook, U.S. Forest Service; Backing Fire Operation, NWCG S-390 course; Torching fire, NWCG S-290 course; Airtanker, NAFRI Images CD-ROM; Crown fire, NWCG S-290 course.*

Preface

The electronic version of this publication can be obtained though the Rocky Mountain Research Station publications web page: http://www.fs.fed.us/rm/pubs/rmrs_gtr253.html. The publication and the program can be downloaded from the BehavePlus section of the website http://www.FireModels.org. This publication is also bundled with the program as the Help system.

Funding for development of the Fire Characteristics Chart program was provided by the USDA Forest Service, Fire and Aviation Management, Washington, DC, and the Rocky Mountain Research Station, Fire, Fuel, and Smoke Program. Programming was done through a contract with Systems for Environmental Management (SEM).

We thank the following reviewers for providing helpful comments on this document and the computer program: William Aney (U.S. Forest Service), Kelly Close (City of Fort Collins, Colorado), Louisa Evers (USDOI Bureau of Land Management), Valentijn Hoff (University of Montana), Tobin Kelley (U.S. Forest Service), Joe Scott (Pyrologix), and Deb Tirmenstein (SEM).

Authors

Patricia L. Andrews is a Research Physical Scientist with the Fire, Fuel, and Smoke Science Program at the Fire Sciences Laboratory in Missoula, Montana. She has been at the Fire Lab since 1973, serving as Project Leader of the Fire Behavior Research Work Unit from 1991 to 1996. Her research focus is fire behavior prediction and fire danger rating.

Faith Ann Heinsch is a post-doctoral Research Ecologist with the Fire, Fuel, and Smoke Science Program at the Fire Sciences Laboratory in Missoula, Montana, where she has focused on improving fire behavior and fire danger modeling systems as well as on climate change. From 2002 to 2008, she worked at the University of Montana with the Numerical Terradynamic Simulation Group (NTSG) in the College of Forestry and Conservation, where she analyzed vegetation productivity in response to current changes in climate and collaborated in climate change research, education, and outreach.

Luke Schelvan is a Software Engineer with Systems for Environmental Management (SEM) in Missoula, Montana. He received a B.S. degree in Computer Science from the University of Montana in 1993. He has been involved in a number of projects related to fire behavior with SEM since 2003.

Contents

1 Introduction

A fire characteristics chart is a graph that illustrates primary fire behavior values—spread rate and intensity. The location of a plotted point represents the character of a fire, which can range from a fast spreading, low intensity fire to a slow spreading, high intensity fire. The chart is a visual aid for displaying both observed fire behavior and values calculated by computer programs such as the BehavePlus fire modeling system (Andrews 2007; Andrews and others 2008).

Graphic presentation of quantitative fire behavior values can support a number of applications. A scientist or student can use the fire characteristics chart to compare predicted and observed fire behavior. A Fire Behavior Analyst can use it to describe potential fire behavior in a briefing to a wildfire management overhead team. A prescribed fire planner can use it to illustrate acceptable fire behavior in a fire prescription document. Anyone can use the fire characteristics chart to better understand fire models by showing the effect of a change in fuel model, fuel moisture, wind speed, or slope on calculated rate of spread, heat per unit area, flame length, and fireline intensity.

Mathematical relationships among rate of spread, heat per unit area, fireline intensity, and flame length are the basis for the surface and crown fire behavior characteristics charts. The surface fire characteristics chart includes curves for several flame length values as related to rate of spread and heat per unit area (Figure 1) with symbols for fire suppression interpretations ranging from fires that can be attacked by persons with hand tools to fires for which control efforts are ineffective. The fire characteristics chart is, therefore, also known as the "hauling chart"— haul in crews, haul in equipment, haul in aircraft, or haul everything out of there. The fire characteristics chart was developed for surface fire behavior by Andrews and Rothermel (1982). Rothermel (1991) later used the concept to develop a crown fire characteristics chart (Figure 2).

The BehavePlus fire modeling system includes an option for producing a fire characteristics chart output for surface fire, with limited capabilities for plotting and labeling. There is not a similar output option for crown fire. The chart that is produced in BehavePlus is only for calculated values and cannot be used to plot observed fire behavior or adjusted calculated values. The computer program described in this report offers plotting flexibility and produces a chart that is suitable for inclusion in briefings, reports, and presentations.

Figure 1—The surface fire behavior fire characteristics chart is used to plot rate of spread, heat per unit area, and flame length for calculated or observed fire behavior (Andrews and Rothermel 1982). Figures on the chart are an indication of fire suppression effectiveness related to flame length.

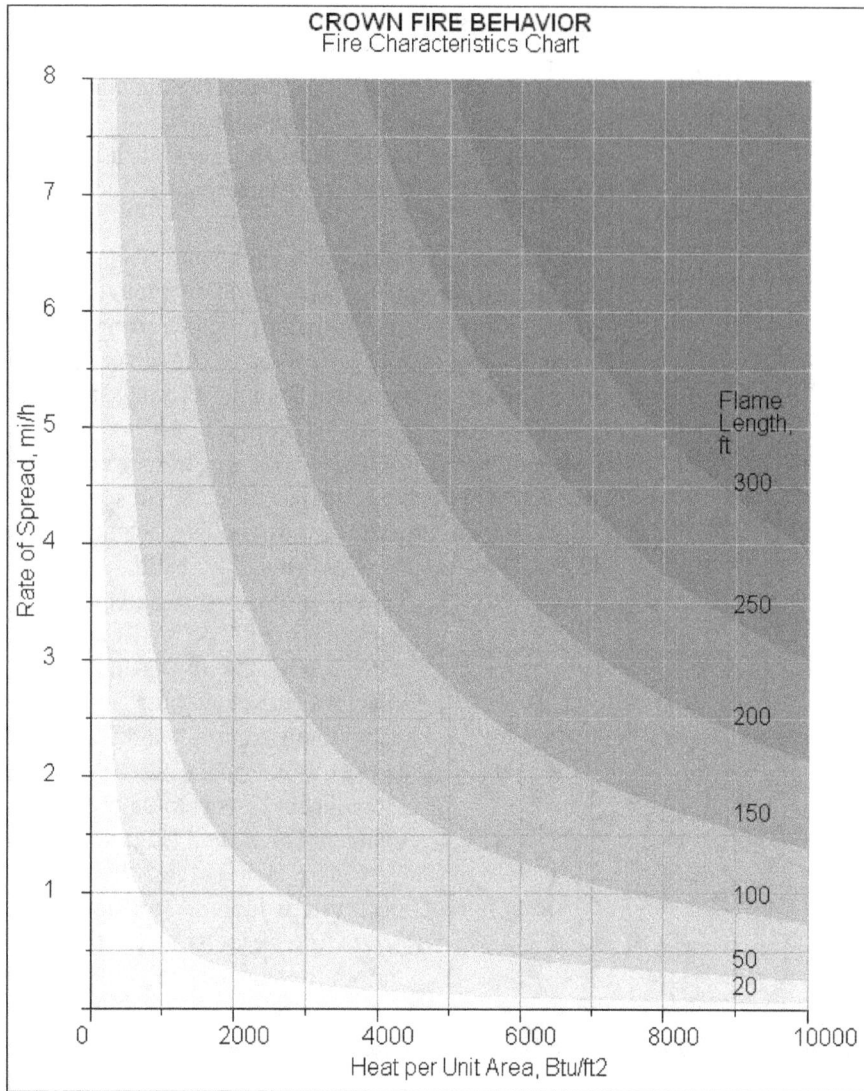

CROWN FIRE BEHAVIOR
Fire Characteristics Chart

Figure 2—The crown fire behavior fire characteristics chart is used to plot rate of spread, heat per unit area, and flame length for calculated or observed crown fire behavior (Rothermel 1991). The crown fire flame length model is different from that used for surface fire.

Figure 3 illustrates the relationship between flame length and fireline intensity. The flame length of a spreading surface fire is the distance between the average tip of the flame and the ground (or surface of the remaining fuel) midway in the active flaming zone. Fireline intensity is the heat energy release per unit time per unit length of fire front. Fireline intensity relates to a foot (or meter) wide section of the fuel bed that extends from the front to the rear of the active flaming zone (Figure 3). Unlike fireline intensity, flame length is an observable characteristic of fire behavior. However, as stated by Rothermel (1991): "Flame length is an elusive parameter that exists in the eye of the beholder. It is a poor quantity to use in a scientific or engineering sense, but it is so readily apparent to fireline personnel and so readily conveys a sense of fire intensity that it is worth featuring as a primary fire variable."

While there is a direct (non-linear) mathematical relationship between fireline intensity and flame length (although different for surface and crown fire), we have chosen to label chart curves with only flame length values.

Flame length and fireline intensity are related to the heat felt by a person standing next to the flames and have been interpreted in terms of suppression capabilities. Figures on the chart aid general interpretation. Table 1 was developed for the advanced fire behavior training course (S-590; Rothermel 1983) and was derived from a more detailed table prepared by Roussopoulos (1974) for a National Fuel Management Workshop (Appendix A). The fireline intensity values in Table 1 are rounded because they are general guidelines.

Four variables are represented by a single point on the chart: rate of spread, heat per unit area, fireline intensity, and flame length. The relationship among these variables is used to produce the surface and crown fire charts; equations are given in the Modeling Foundation section. While four values are represented by a given point, only two values are specified to locate the plotted point: rate of spread (ROS) and either flame length (FL) or heat per unit area (HPUA). When plotting was done with a pencil on a paper chart, it was easiest to enter values for the X- and Y-axes, HPUA and ROS, because it is difficult to estimate the correct location of a flame length value between the curves. A computer can easily plot a point given ROS and FL, which are the more likely available values for fire behavior observations.

USDA Forest Service Gen. Tech. Rep. RMRS-GTR-253. 2011

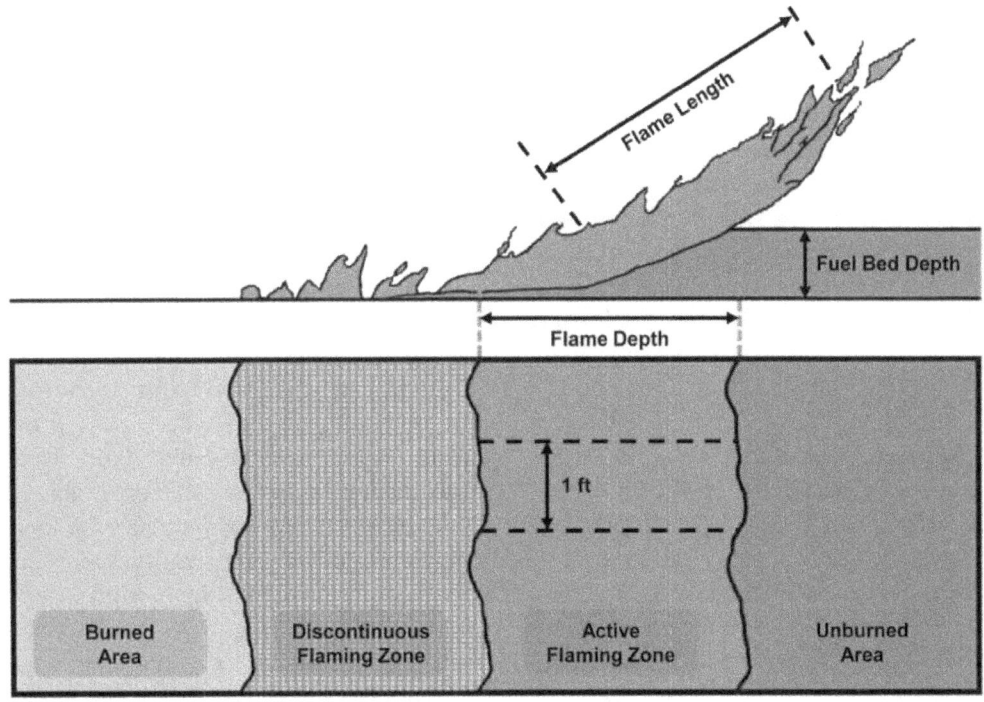

Figure 3—The diagrams illustrate the relationship between flame length and fireline intensity. A side view of a wind-driven fire shows that flame length is measured from midway in the active flaming zone to the average tip of the flames. The overhead view illustrates that fireline intensity is the heat energy release per unit time from a foot (or meter) wide section of the fuel bed extending from the front to the rear of the active flaming zone.

Table 1—Relationship of surface fire flame length and fireline intensity to suppression interpretations.

Flame length		Fireline intensity		Interpretation	
ft	m	Btu/ft/s	kJ/m/s		
< 4	< 1.2	< 100	<350		• Fires can generally be attacked at the head or flanks by persons using hand tools. • Hand line should hold the fire.
4 – 8	1.2 – 2.4	100 – 500	350 – 1700		• Fires are too intense for direct attack on the head by persons using hand tools. • Hand line cannot be relied on to hold the fire. • Equipment such as dozers, pumpers, and retardant aircraft can be effective.
8 – 11	2.4 – 3.4	500 – 1000	1700 – 3500		• Fires may present serious control problems—torching out, crowning, and spotting. • Control efforts at the fire head will probably be ineffective
> 11	> 3.4	> 1000	> 3500		• Crowning, spotting, and major fire runs are probable. • Control efforts at head of fire are ineffective.

In simplified terms, heat per unit area is equal to the fireline intensity divided by rate of spread. Heat per unit area is the heat release for an *area*. Fireline intensity is a heat release *rate*. For any given fireline intensity (flame length), the faster the rate of spread, the less heat will be directed to the site. Conversely, a slow-moving fire with the same fireline intensity as a fast-moving fire will concentrate considerable heat on the site (Rothermel and Deeming 1980).

The surface fire characteristics chart has a much lower range of spread rate and intensity than the crown fire characteristics chart. The surface fire chart depicts the limits of fire control as well as general guidelines for torching and crown fire development. These limits are all exceeded by active crown fires. A crown fire should always be considered uncontrollable by direct attack at the head of the fire.

Because the model for crown fire flame length is different from that used for surface fire flame length, we do not combine the two fire types on a single fire characteristics chart. A fireline intensity of 1000 Btu/ft/s produced by a surface fire gives a flame length of approximately 11 ft, whereas that same intensity generates a flame length of approximately 20 ft for a crown fire. Details are provided in the Modeling Foundation section. A common chart could be used if the curves were labeled only with fireline intensity and were not labeled as or interpreted in terms of flame length. We do not offer that option in our program because it would be contrary to the primary purpose of the chart—a visual comparison of fire characteristics. As noted earlier, it is easier to visualize the character of a fire in terms of flame length rather than fireline intensity.

As an example of the information that can be gained from viewing plotted values on a fire characteristics chart, we compare calculated fire behavior for four fuel models under the same environmental conditions. A BehavePlus run was produced for fuel models 1, 10, 8, and 4 for 5 percent dead fuel moisture, 100 percent live fuel moisture, midflame wind speed of 7 mi/h, and 10 percent slope (Figure 4). As described by Anderson (1982), fuel model 1 can represent continuous stands of arid western grass; fuel model 10—the litter and

Figure 4—A BehavePlus run with values for four fuel models to be plotted on the surface fire characteristics chart.

understory of a timber stand with heavy accumulations of deadfall; fuel model 8—short needle litter; and fuel model 4—chaparral. Fuel models 1 and 8 include only dead fuel. A look at the BehavePlus table output shows a significant difference in calculated rate of spread, heat per unit area, fireline intensity, and flame length for the four fuel models.

Plotting calculated values on the fire characteristics chart (Figure 5) provides a visual display of fire characteristics and the relationship among the fire behavior values for the four modeled fires. The flame length is roughly 6.5 ft for both fuel models 1 and 10 under the stated moisture, wind, and slope conditions. According to the interpretations in Table 1, both fires may be too intense for direct attack at the head by persons using hand tools. The character of the two fires is, however, very different. The fire in fuel model 1 (short grass) is fast spreading with a low heat per unit area, while the fire in fuel model 10 (timber litter and understory) is slow spreading with a high heat per unit area. While the fireline intensity is nearly identical (about 340 Btu/ft/s) for fuel models 1 and 10 under these conditions, the large difference in heat per unit area (32 Btu/ft^2 and 1330 Btu/ft^2) results from the much faster fire rate of spread in fuel model 1, which produces much less heat at any given point on the ground.

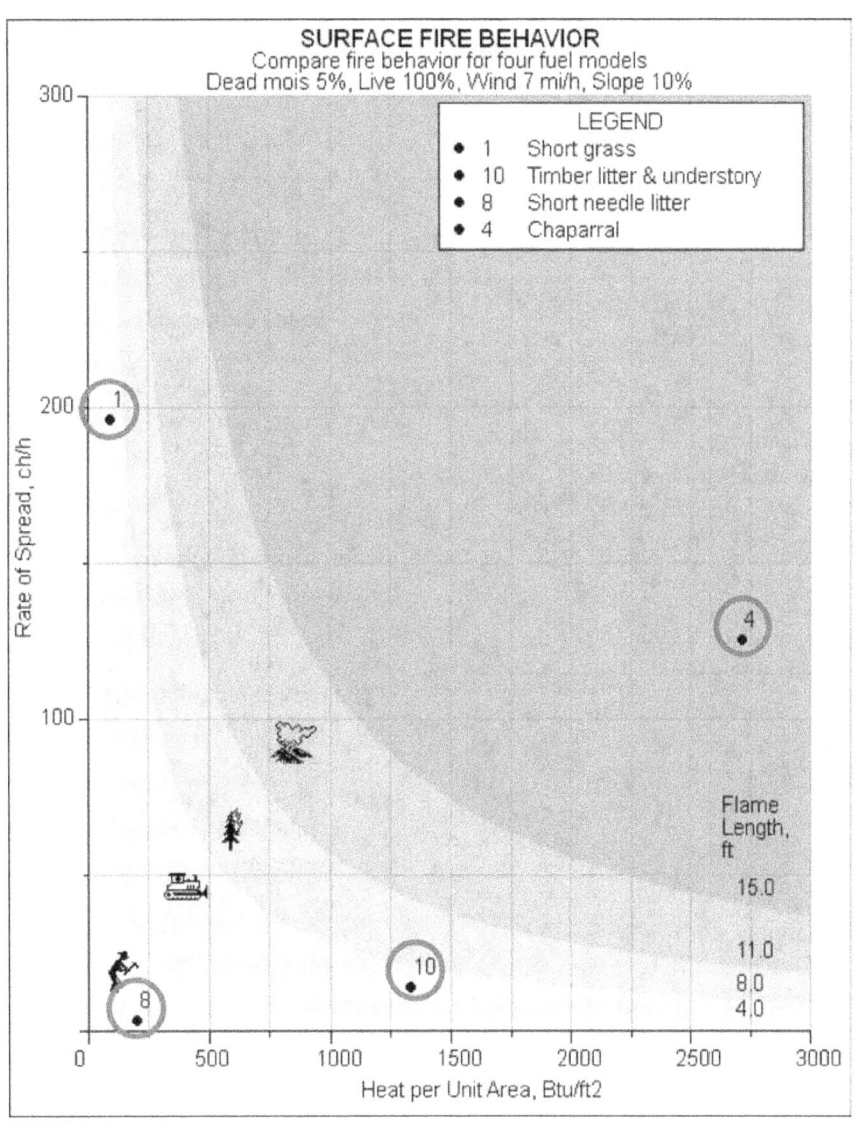

Figure 5—Outputs from the BehavePlus run in Figure 4 are plotted on the fire characteristics chart.

USDA Forest Service Gen. Tech. Rep. RMRS-GTR-253. 2011

5

A fire in fuel model 8 (short needle litter) under the same environmental conditions has both a low spread rate and low heat per unit area. The calculated flame length is 1.5 ft, indicating that it may be controlled by hand crews. The other extreme is the fire in fuel model 4 (chaparral), which has a high spread rate and a high heat per unit area. The calculated flame length of more than 25 ft means control efforts at the fire head would be ineffective.

The plotted points in Figure 5 are circled for emphasis (added to the chart produced by our program, using other software). The circles might also serve as a reminder of the inherent variability of wildland fire, as well as the limitations of fire modeling—of the fire models; of the fuel description; and of the fuel moisture, wind, and slope values. Keep in mind that the guidance given in training courses that use nomograms to predict fire behavior (Albini 1976b) has been to use a fat crayon rather than a sharp pencil (Rothermel 2009). This also applies to the fire characteristics chart.

We have described what a fire characteristics chart is and have given an example of how the character of four modeled fires can be compared using the chart. The remainder of this paper is organized into three sections.

- **Applications**. Examples of use of the chart are given, with focus on application rather than on methods of producing the charts.
- **Program Operation**. Program use and available options are detailed in the form of a reference guide.
- **Modeling Foundation**. The mathematical relationships that form the foundation of the fire characteristics charts are described. Other forms of the fire characteristics chart are briefly described.

2 Applications _____

Using the fire characteristics chart to visually display quantitative fire behavior values (observations, calculations, or adjusted calculations) can be useful for many applications.

We present example applications of a fire characteristics chart for the following:

- Fire model understanding
- Documentation of observed fire behavior
- Illustration of the effect of ignition pattern on prescribed fire behavior
- Comparison of fire behavior within and outside of a prescribed fire unit
- Briefings to a fire management overhead team
- Case studies and after action reviews

These examples demonstrate various format options that are offered by the program. In some cases, we have used additional software to add text and figures to the charts.

2.1 Fire Model Understanding

The fire characteristics chart program does not include fire model calculations; observed values or values that are calculated using any fire behavior modeling software can be entered and plotted. The display of relationships among calculated values can aid fire model understanding. In addition to personal use, the fire characteristics chart can help in formal training sessions that describe relationships of input variables to calculated fire behavior.

In the Introduction, we compared surface fire behavior for four fuel models under the same environmental conditions. In the following examples, we first compare the effect of live fuel moisture for two fuel models. We then compare crown fire behavior for two values of canopy bulk density and wind speed. In both examples, we display calculations from BehavePlus.

2.1.1 Surface Fire—Effect of Live Fuel Moisture

The BehavePlus run in Figure 6 is for two grass fuel models and two values of live fuel moisture. Figure 7 shows the four points plotted on a fire characteristics chart. This is a simple comparison of modeled fire behavior for fuel models 2 and GR2 with 50 percent and 100 percent live fuel moisture, 5 percent dead fuel moisture, midflame wind speed of 5 mi/h, and 0 percent slope. Fuel model 2 (timber grass and understory) is one of the 13 fuel models described by Anderson (1982). Fuel model GR2 (low load, dry climate grass) is one of the 40 fuel models developed by Scott and Burgan (2005).

The fire characteristics chart illustrates that the change in live fuel moisture results in a greater change in fire behavior for fuel model 2 than for fuel model GR2. This is in large part because fuel model 2 is static and GR2 is dynamic. The parameters of a static fuel model do not change. A dynamic fuel model, on the other hand, is designed to reflect seasonal changes in fuel loading due to curing. The fuel model parameters of a dynamic fuel model change as a function of live herbaceous fuel moisture; fuel load is transferred from the live to the dead category. At 100 percent, most of the live herbaceous fuel is not cured (in other words, it is still considered live fuel). At a fuel moisture of 50 percent, most of the fuel is cured, meaning most of the live herbaceous fuel load has been transferred to the dead category. Live herbaceous fuel moisture influences calculated fire behavior for both fuel model 2 and GR2. There is an additional influence on GR2 due to the load transfer function, resulting in the differences shown in Figures 6 and 7.

The purpose of this example is to compare changes in fire behavior that result from a change in input. Because the objective is not fire suppression interpretation, the suppression icons were removed and the flame length curves were changed, (compare with the basic chart in Figure 1). Chart scales were changed to better display plotted points, and we used other software to add dashed lines to emphasize relationships.

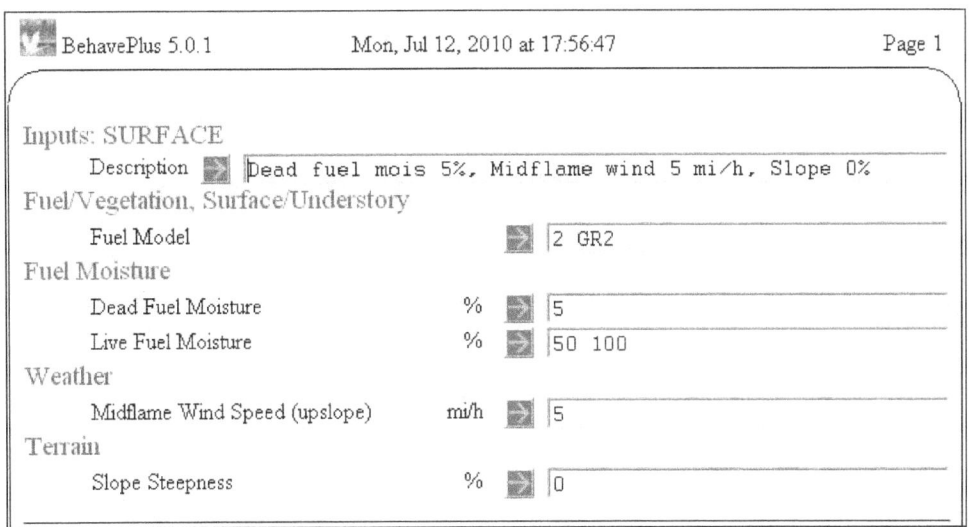

Figure 6—BehavePlus input and table output. The same live moisture value is used for live woody and herbaceous fuel. Fuel model 2 is static and GR2 is dynamic.

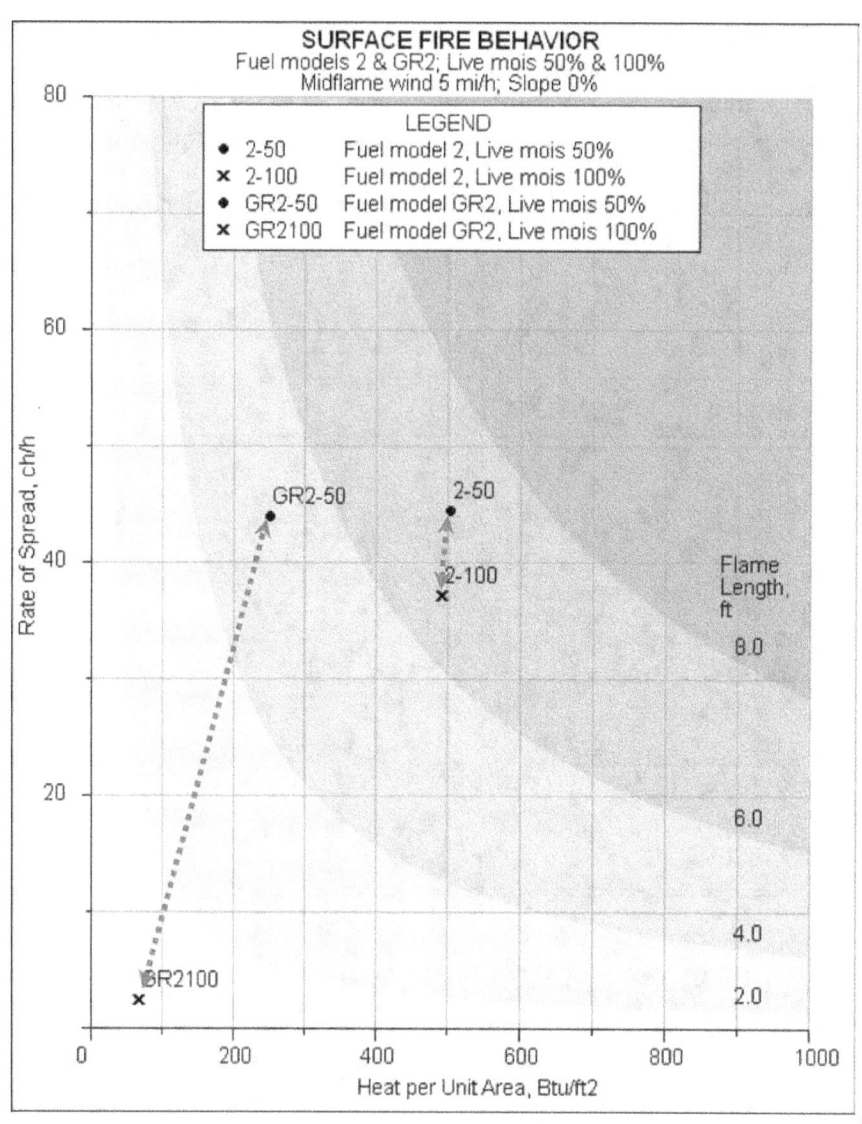

Figure 7—Plotted points compare fuel models 2 and GR2 for live fuel moistures of 50% and 100%. Other conditions are constant. BehavePlus calculations are shown in Figure 6.

2.1.2 Crown Fire—Effect of Canopy Base Height, Canopy Bulk Density, and Wind Speed

Results of BehavePlus runs (Figure 8) show an example of the effect of canopy base height (CBH), canopy bulk density (CBD), and 10-m wind speed on crown fire behavior. The associated fire characteristics chart is in Figure 9. Metric units were selected for both the BehavePlus calculations and the chart.

Because we are demonstrating an application of model understanding rather than a complete analysis of fire behavior, the BehavePlus run was limited to calculation of crown fire rate of spread, heat per unit area, flame length, and fireline intensity. We did not model surface fire behavior or fire type based on transition to crown fire

and potential for active crown fire. Heat per unit area for the surface fire is, therefore, a user input, selected from a table of values from Rothermel (1991) to represent fuel model 9 (long needle litter) with additional fuel load, as described in the Modeling Foundation section.

Notice that crown rate of spread is influenced by wind speed but not by canopy bulk density or canopy base height. The opposite is the case for heat per unit area, which is influenced by canopy bulk density and canopy base height and not by wind speed. Flame length and fireline intensity are affected by all three variables included in the calculations. Relationships among all crown fire model variables in BehavePlus are available in flowcharts in the Help window.

Inputs: CROWN

Description ➡ Canopy Base Ht = 5 m

Fuel/Vegetation, Overstory

Canopy Height	m	➡	15
Canopy Base Height	m	➡	5
Canopy Bulk Density	kg/m3	➡	.1 .2

Fuel Moisture

1-h Moisture	%	➡	4
10-h Moisture	%	➡	4
100-h Moisture	%	➡	4
Live Woody Moisture	%	➡	70

Weather

10-m Wind Speed	km/h	➡	40 80

Fire

Heat per Unit Area	kJ/m2	➡	15059

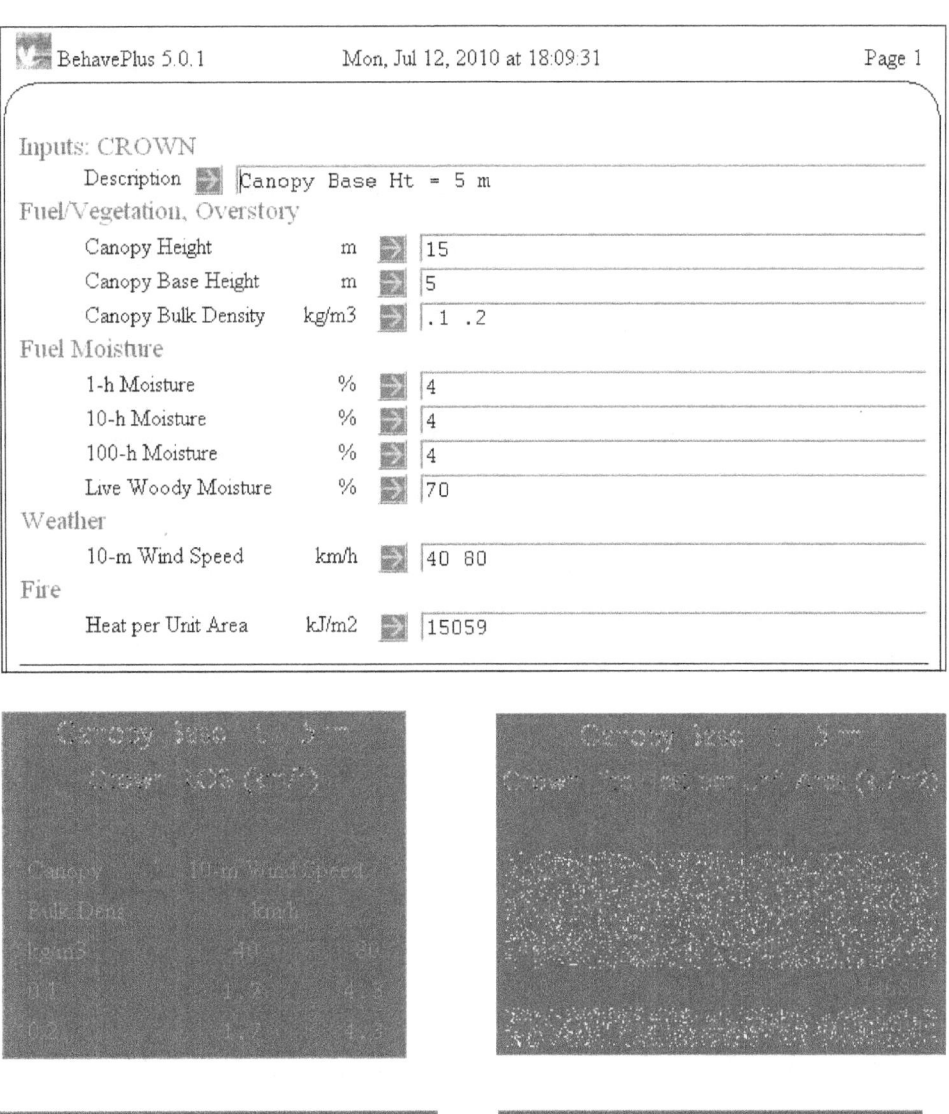

Figure 8—BehavePlus runs producing crown fire behavior values that are plotted on the fire characteristics chart in Figure 9.

(continued)

Figure 8—(continued)

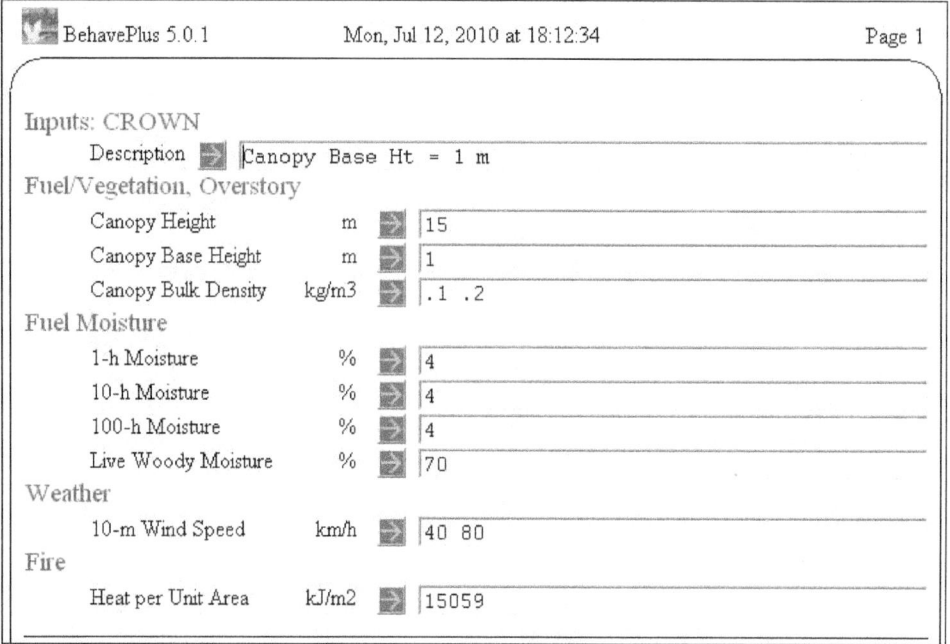

| BehavePlus 5.0.1 | Mon, Jul 12, 2010 at 18:12:34 | Page 1 |

Inputs: CROWN

Description → Canopy Base Ht = 1 m

Fuel/Vegetation, Overstory

Canopy Height	m	→	15
Canopy Base Height	m	→	1
Canopy Bulk Density	kg/m3	→	.1 .2

Fuel Moisture

1-h Moisture	%	→	4
10-h Moisture	%	→	4
100-h Moisture	%	→	4
Live Woody Moisture	%	→	70

Weather

| 10-m Wind Speed | km/h | → | 40 80 |

Fire

| Heat per Unit Area | kJ/m2 | → | 15059 |

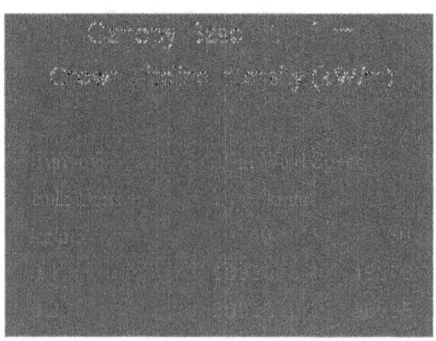

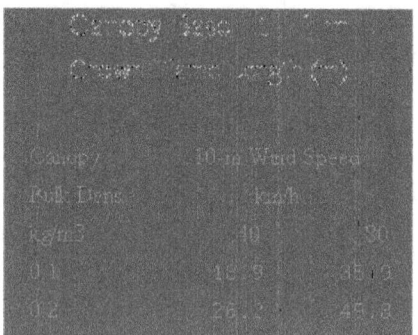

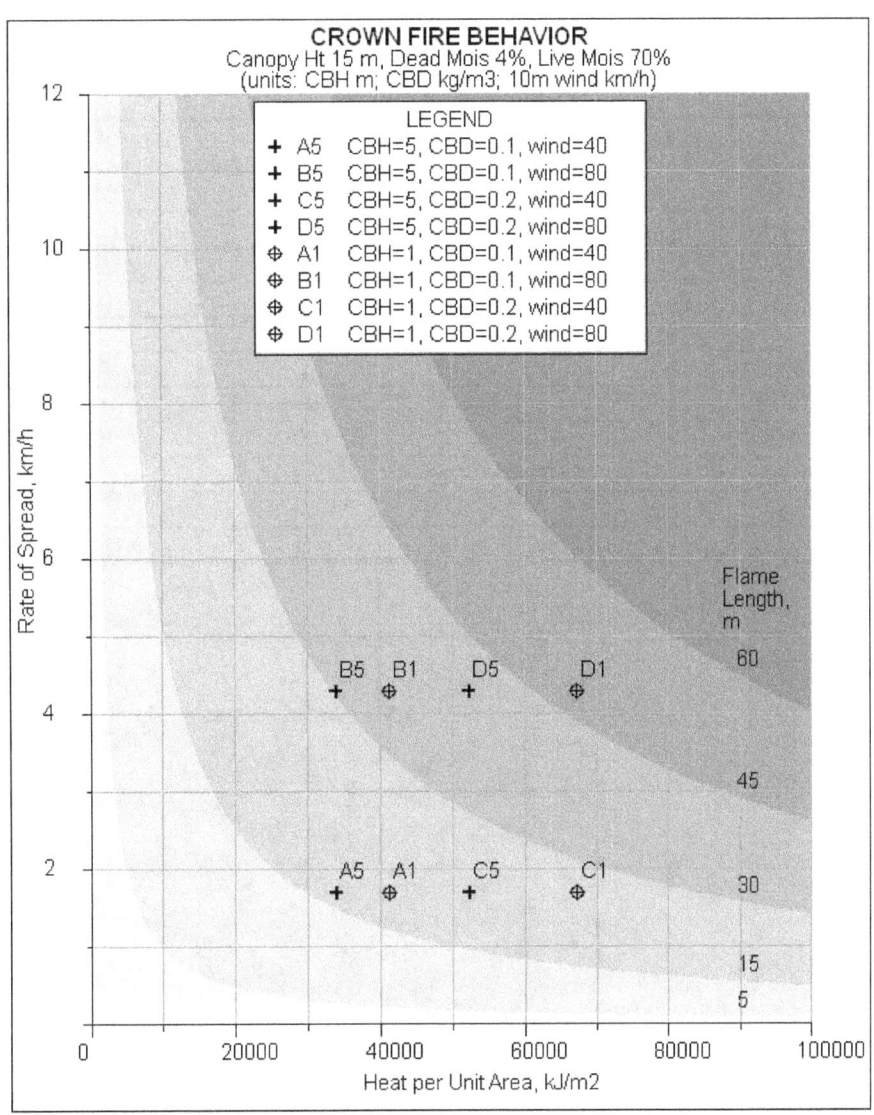

Figure 9—Plotted points from BehavePlus calculations (Figure 8) show difference in fire characteristics resulting from varying wind speeds and canopy bulk density.

2.2 Observed Crown Fire Behavior

Anderson (1968) documented the Sundance Fire that burned across northern Idaho in 1967. It burned in mixed conifers, was driven by winds of up to 45 mi/h, and reached spread rates of 6 mi/h. The magnitude of the fire resulted from a prolonged dry period, persistent high temperatures, sustained winds during the fire run, and an uncontrolled 4-mile fire front. In a period of 9 hours, the fire traveled 16 miles and burned more than 50,000 acres.

The major fire run occurred on September 1, 1967, from approximately 1400 to 2300. Observed rates of spread and calculated fireline intensity values were taken from Anderson (1968) and are given in Table 2. Flame length values were calculated for this table using the Thomas (1963) model (equation 10). Rate of spread and flame length values were plotted on the fire characteristics chart (Figure 10). Other software was used to connect the points to show the envelope of fire behavior during the run.

USDA Forest Service Gen. Tech. Rep. RMRS-GTR-253. 2011

11

Table 2—Hourly rate of spread and fireline intensity of the Sundance Fire on September 1, 1967, from Anderson (1968). Flame length values were calculated for this table based on Thomas (1963).

Time	Rate of spread, mi/h	Fireline intensity, Btu/ft/s	Flame length, ft
1400	0.75	1000	20
1500	1.25	5400	62
1600	1.6	6900	72
1700	<1.0	3150	43
1800	2.5	11,300	101
1900	1	3400	45
2000	6	22,500	159
2100	2.5	8250	82
2200	1.5	3800	49
2300	0.5	735	16

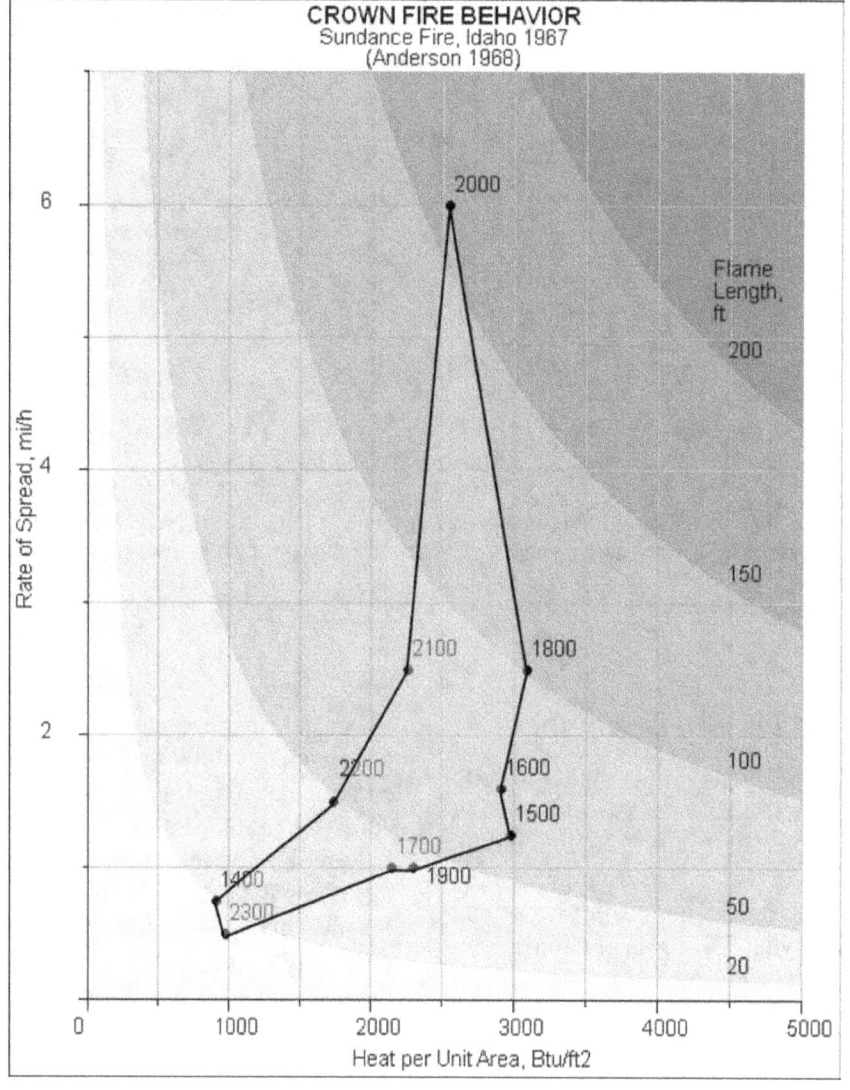

Figure 10—Envelope of the observed behavior of the Sundance Fire by time of day for September 1, 1967. Plotted values (rate of spread and flame length) are from Table 2.

USDA Forest Service Gen. Tech. Rep. RMRS-GTR-253. 2011

2.3 Ignition Pattern Effect on Fire Behavior

The Rothermel surface fire spread model is based on the assumption that fire is steady-state, burning under uniform conditions. This is not the case for prescribed fire where the pattern of ignition is used to affect fire behavior. Rothermel (1984) discussed applying fire model predictions to this situation, stating that "Prediction of fire behavior is difficult, but careful and selected use of available methods can aid planning and execution of prescribed fire by aerial ignition or other ignition methods." He used the fire characteristics chart to illustrate differences between the steady-state fire behavior calculated by the model and fire with (1) lesser fire behavior that had not reached steady-state, and (2) greater fire behavior driven by induced winds.

Fire characteristics charts might be included in a burn plan to show the calculated steady-state behavior and the behavior that is planned via ignition pattern. Calculated values using ambient conditions can be plotted, illustrating expected behavior if the fire were allowed to reach steady-state, without induced winds on the fire. In addition, a calculation with no wind can represent a lower limit for fire behavior. If narrow strips are used and ignition of successive strips is delayed until the fine fuel has burned, the expected rate of spread and flame length should lie somewhere between the two points. Faster spread rates and larger flames can be achieved by more rapid ignition of strips that are spread wide enough to allow flames to fully develop but not so wide as to get beyond the indraft influence. The upper limit of fire behavior is unknown since it is determined by the amount of induced wind that is generated by the ignition system and the heat generation of the fire. However, the effect of induced wind can be indicated on the chart above the calculated values.

The following two examples are based on those presented by Rothermel (1984). BehavePlus was used to do the calculations. We used other software to highlight plotted points and to add labels.

Suppose there is a scheduled burn in sagebrush. A high pressure system is stagnant over the area, producing warm weather but no wind. From experience and/or test fires, it is known that the fuel is too sparse to burn without an 8- to 10-mi/h wind. The calculated no-wind behavior and the value plotted on the fire characteristics chart are shown in Figure 11. Even though the heat per unit area is considerable (656 Btu/ft^2), the rate of spread is very low (1.2 ch/h) and, as noted, the fire won't actually spread under no-wind conditions. If induced winds of 8 to 10 mi/h can be generated using rapid, aerial ignition, the fire would plot as shown on the chart. The fireline intensity would increase significantly and the flame lengths would range between 8 and 10 ft.

As a second example, suppose there is an area on a 30 percent slope with fuels represented by fuel model 12 (medium slash). The dead and down fuel load could be a result of logging or of blow-down following beetle kill. The burn is planned for the afternoon, when dead fuel moisture nears 7 percent. Upslope winds are predicted to be about 5 mi/h at eye level (midflame). A helitorch will be used for strip ignition, and we would like to assess expected fire behavior.

The effect of induced wind can be illustrated on the fire characteristics chart by calculating fire behavior for a no-wind condition and for a 5 mi/h midflame wind. Both of these conditions are plotted on the chart in Figure 12. The ambient wind condition indicates the expected behavior if there are no induced winds on the fire. The no-wind condition indicates behavior if the fire were backing down the slope.

If the strips are kept narrow and ignition of successive strips is delayed until the fine fuel has burned out, the expected rate of spread and flame length should lie in the bracketed area marked "narrow strips" between the two points. The effect of induced wind is located above the other two points on the chart, as shown by the arrow.

2.4 Prescribed Fire Plan

The Interagency Prescribed Fire Guide (USDA and USDOI 2008) defines *prescription* as "the measureable criteria that define a range of conditions during which a prescribed fire may be ignited and held as a prescribed fire." In addition to specifying acceptable fire behavior within the burn unit, the guide states: "Holding and contingency plans must be developed with the consideration of the predicted fire behavior outside the project boundary(s). Fire behavior characteristics for fuel models within the maximum spotting distance and/or adjacent to the project boundaries must be considered and modeled."

While the fire behavior within a prescribed fire burn unit may be controlled by the pattern of ignition, a spot fire outside of the unit would better meet the steady-state assumptions of the fire model. The fire characteristics chart can illustrate differences in fire behavior that result from different conditions inside and outside of the unit. Surface fuel models and slope may differ; dead fuel moisture will depend on aspect and overstory shading; live fuel moisture will depend on aspect and vegetation type; and midflame wind speed will depend on overstory sheltering.

USDA Forest Service Gen. Tech. Rep. RMRS-GTR-253. 2011

13

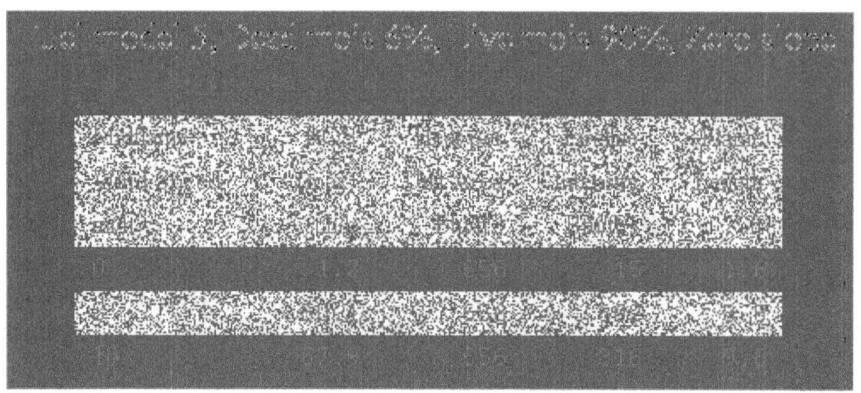

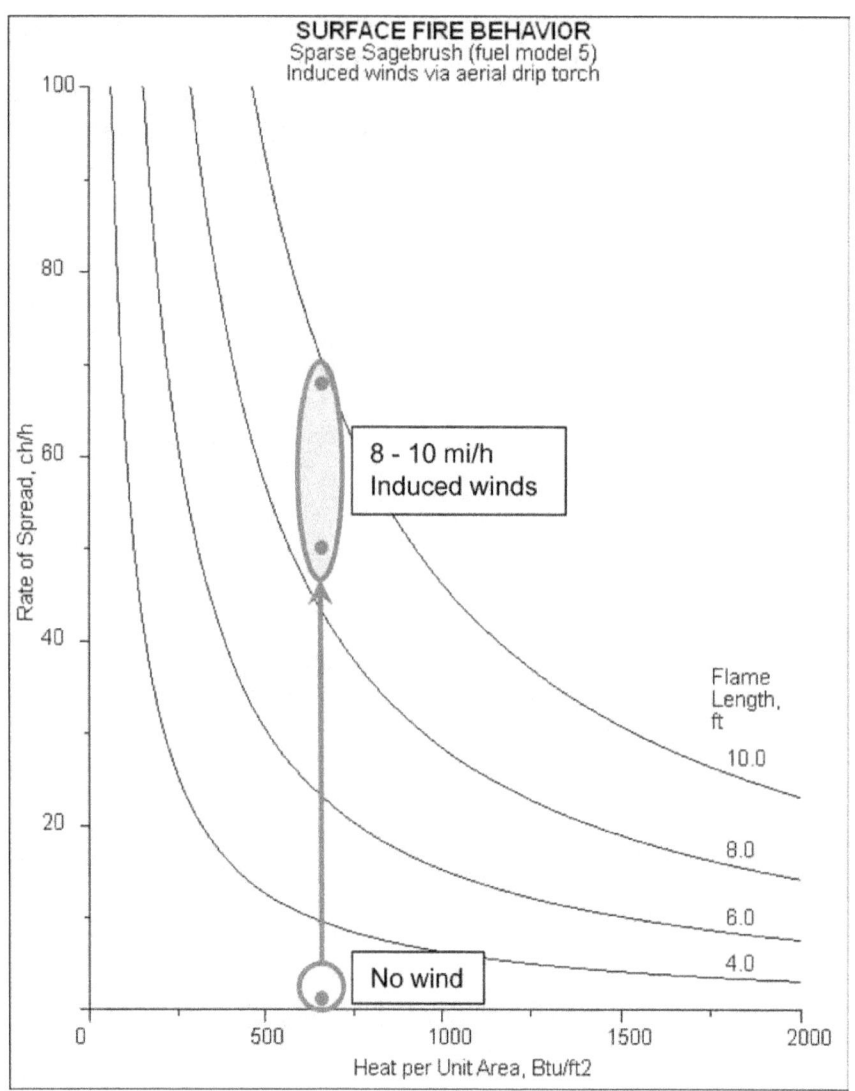

Figure 11—Effect of induced winds on sagebrush fire characteristics (based on Rothermel 1984).

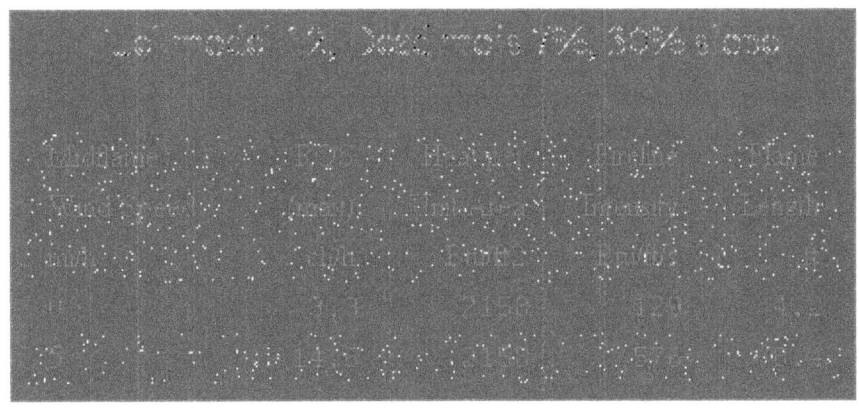

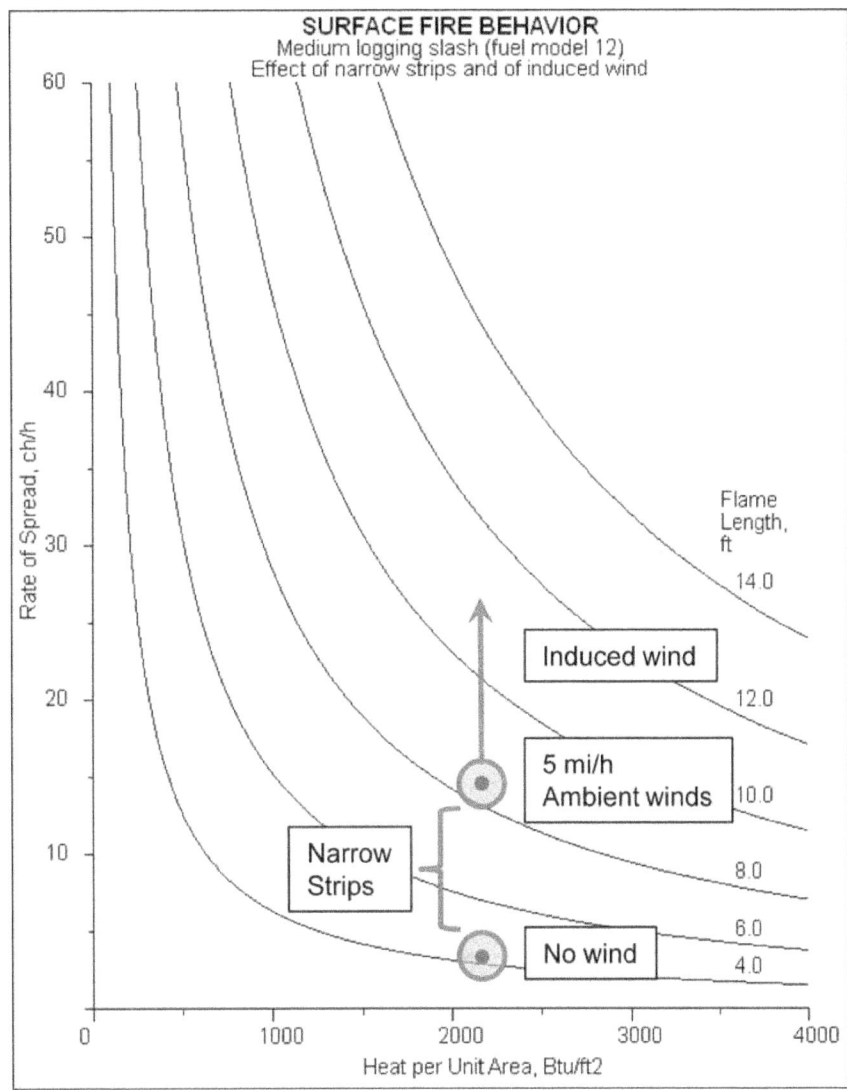

Figure 12—Effect of narrow strips and of induced winds on logging slash fire characteristics (based on Rothermel 1984).

Figure 13 is a map of a burn unit with labeled fuel models for the surrounding area and calculated maximum spotting distance. Table 3 gives calculated rate of spread and flame length of fire within the unit and of potential spot fires outside the unit. Calculations for fire within the unit are done for fuel model 11 (light logging slash) with a 20-ft wind speed of 25 mi/h and zero wind. The ignition plan will not allow the fire to reach the maximum steady-state spread rate.

Fire behavior is calculated for litter fuel models TL2 and TL6 in addition to fuel model 9 (long needle litter), which is shown on the map.

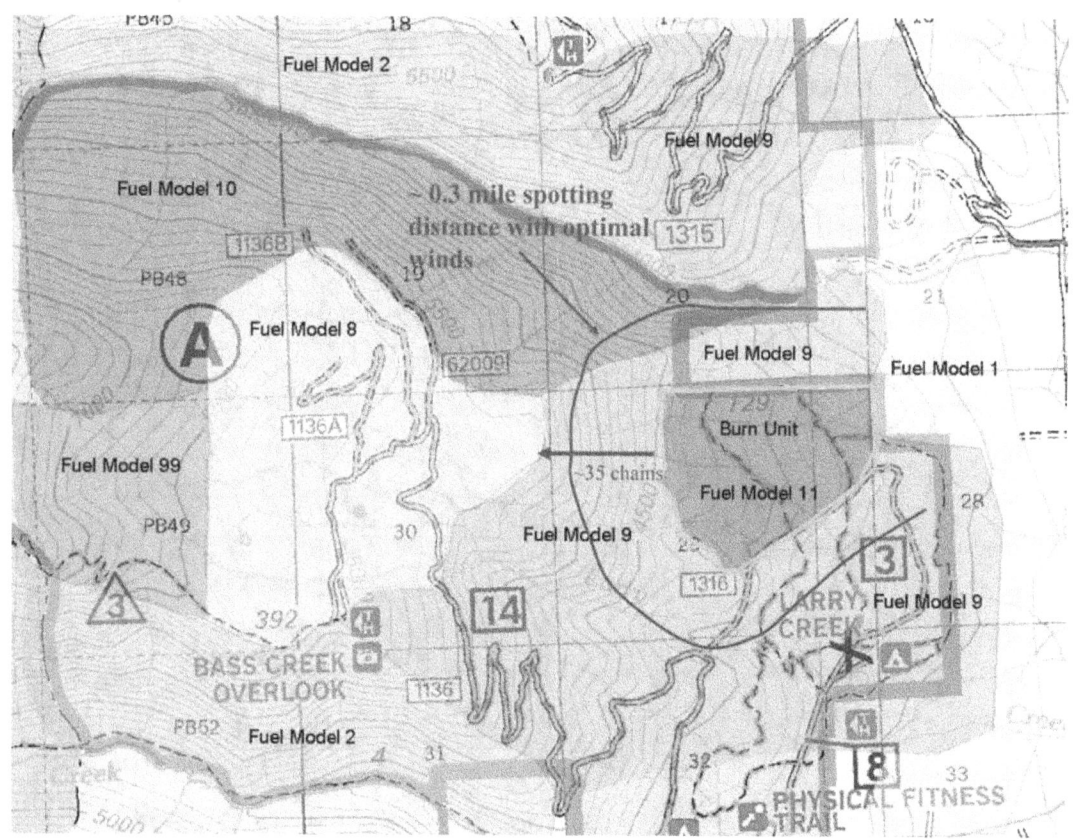

Figure 13—Map showing the relationship of the burn unit (fuel model 11) to areas and associated fuel models outside of the unit. The calculated maximum spotting distance is indicated (developed by Tobin Kelley, U.S. Forest Service).

Table 3—Conditions and calculated fire behavior for within the burn unit (fuel model 11) and for potential spot fires outside of the burn unit.

Fuel model	Max slope, %	20-ft wind, mi/h	Wind adj. factor	Midflame wind, mi/h	Dead moist.,* %	Live moist., %	Rate of spread, ch/h	Flame length, ft
11	35	25	0.4	10	5,8,10	—	14.8	5.2
11	35	0	0.4	0.0	5,8,10	—	1.9	2.0
9	45	25	0.3	7.5	7,8,10	—	18.0	4.0
TL2	45	25	0.3	7.5	7,8,10	—	1.9	0.9
TL6	45	25	0.3	7.5	7,8,10	—	11.6	3.6
8	20	25	0.2	5.0	7,8,10	—	2.0	1.1
10	45	25	0.2	5.0	7,8,10	100	10.9	5.0

*1-h, 10-h, 100-h moisture

Figure 14 is a fire characteristics chart that might be included in the prescribed fire plan with the map, description of conditions, and assumptions used in the modeling. Lines were added to the chart to highlight the range of potential fire behavior inside and outside the unit. The scale was changed to better display the plotted points. Because fire suppression interpretation is relevant to this application, the flame length curves and icons were not changed.

2.5 Briefings

Wildland fire behavior information is needed in a variety of settings and is often presented in the form of briefings. The following is taken from a lesson in the S-590 Advanced Fire Behavior Interpretations course: "High quality visual aids help increase the interest of the audience, increase the understanding and retention of information, and can greatly increase the amount of information presented and understood in a shorter

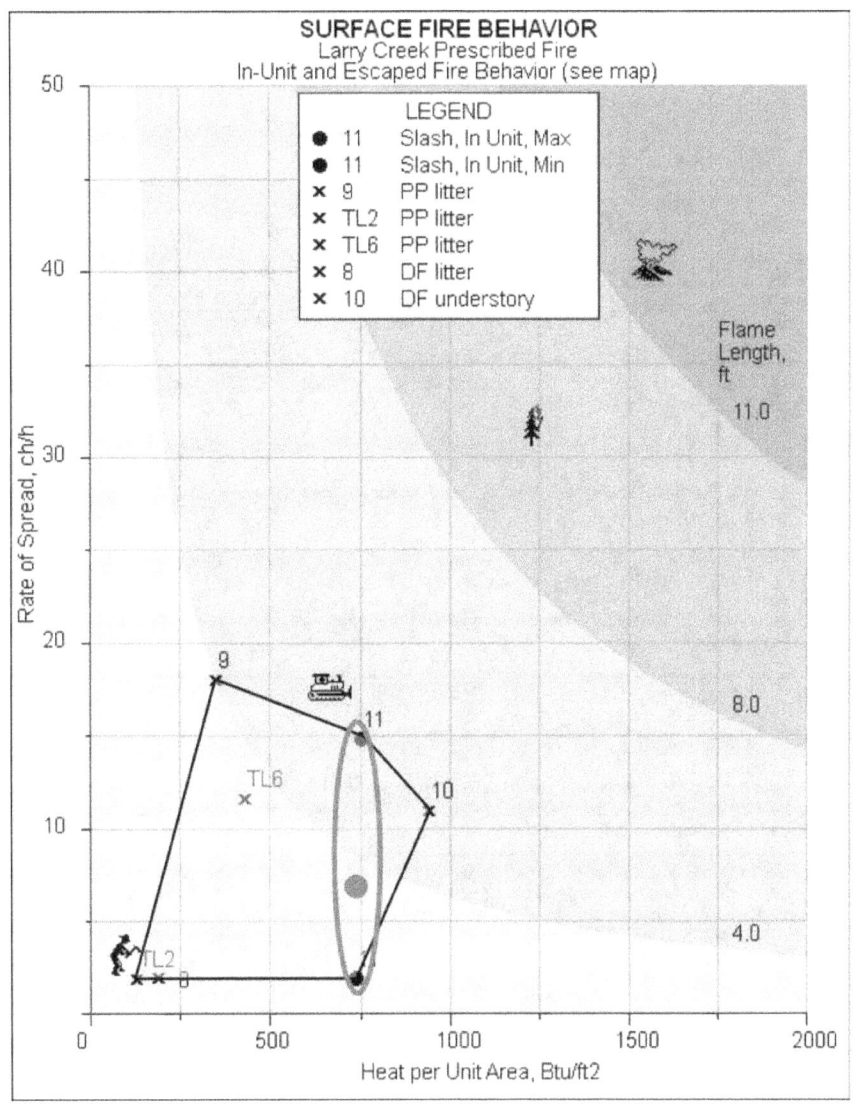

Figure 14—Plot of potential fire behavior of a spot fire outside the burn area and the range of fire behavior in the unit. The ignition method will not allow the prescribed fire to reach steady-state. The planned fire behavior is indicated by the large red dot. The range of potential fire behavior inside and outside the unit is indicated by the shaded envelope.

USDA Forest Service Gen. Tech. Rep. RMRS-GTR-253. 2011

17

period of time. Good visual aids also help present a professional image."

Expected fire behavior by time and location can be illustrated on a fire characteristics chart. A fire behavior forecast can include calculations from a system such as BehavePlus, but the Fire Behavior Analyst also uses observed fire behavior and personal experience to make predictions.

Figure 15 is a portion of a written fire behavior forecast that describes expected fire behavior for the head and flanking fire. Figure 16 shows those values on a fire characteristics chart.

2.6 Case Studies and After Action Reviews

Post-fire documentation, case studies of wildfire behavior, and after action reviews (AAR) of planned and unplanned fires can include a fire characteristics chart. We present an example from the report on the 1989 Black Tiger Fire near Boulder, Colorado (National Fire Protection Association 1990). Rates of spread were determined from the timed progress of the fire as noted from aerial observation. The term "energy density" in that report is equivalent to "heat per unit area" (HPUA) used here. HPUA was estimated for ponderosa pine, mixed conifer, and dry meadow and then fireline intensity was calculated.

FIRE BEHAVIOR FORECAST

FORECAST NUMBER 1	TYPE OF FIRE Wildland Fire Use
FIRE NAME Foot Fire	OPERATIONAL PERIOD 6/17 – 18/92
DATE ISSUED 6/17/92	TIME ISSUED 1600 hrs.
UNIT Everglades National Park	SIGNED /s/ Your Name

INPUTS

WEATHER SUMMARY

Large scale circulation patterns indicate summer weather patterns with increased moisture has begun.

Today: Partly cloudy, 40% chance of showers and thundershowers, maximum temperature of 90, minimum RH 54%, eye-level winds east at 6mph.

Tonight: Partly cloudy, maximum RH of 95%, minimum temperature of 78, mid-flame winds south at 0-1mph. Continued chances of showers and thundershowers (40%)

Tomorrow: Partly cloudy with 60% chance of showers and thundershowers, maximum temperature 88, minimum RH 60%, eye- level winds east at 5mph.

OUTPUTS

FIRE BEHAVIOR

GENERAL

Fire is burning in 6 foot tall sawgrass. Fire will continue to burn actively during the 1st burning period with fire spread being wind driven to the west by afternoon sea breeze. Thunderstorm activity in the area can overpower the sea breeze winds and cause fire spread in any direction.

During daylight hours, expect forward rates of spread up to 55 chains per hour with flame lengths of 12-14 feet at the head. Rates of spread on the flanks will be 4-5 chains per hour with flame lengths of 4-5 feet. Rates of spread on the heel of the fire will be 2-3 chains per hour with flame lengths of 3 feet. Higher rates of spread can be expected on all sides of the fire where thunderstorm downdrafts occur. While spotting could occur up to .4 mile, probability of ignition of 45-50% will limit concern for spotting problems.

Higher relative humidity after sunset will halt fire growth as fuels reach moisture of extinction. Fire may hold over in heavy fuels (thick grass), providing sources for further fire spread tomorrow as conditions dry into the morning. Fire behavior tomorrow will be similar to today where holdovers occur. Natural barriers of Shark and East Sloughs are expected to contain fire. Timbered ridges and roughs burned within the last 12 months will slow or stop fire spread

Figure 15—Portion of a Fire Behavior Forecast prepared by a Fire Behavior Analyst on a wildfire. Expected fire behavior is plotted on the fire characteristics chart in Figure 16.

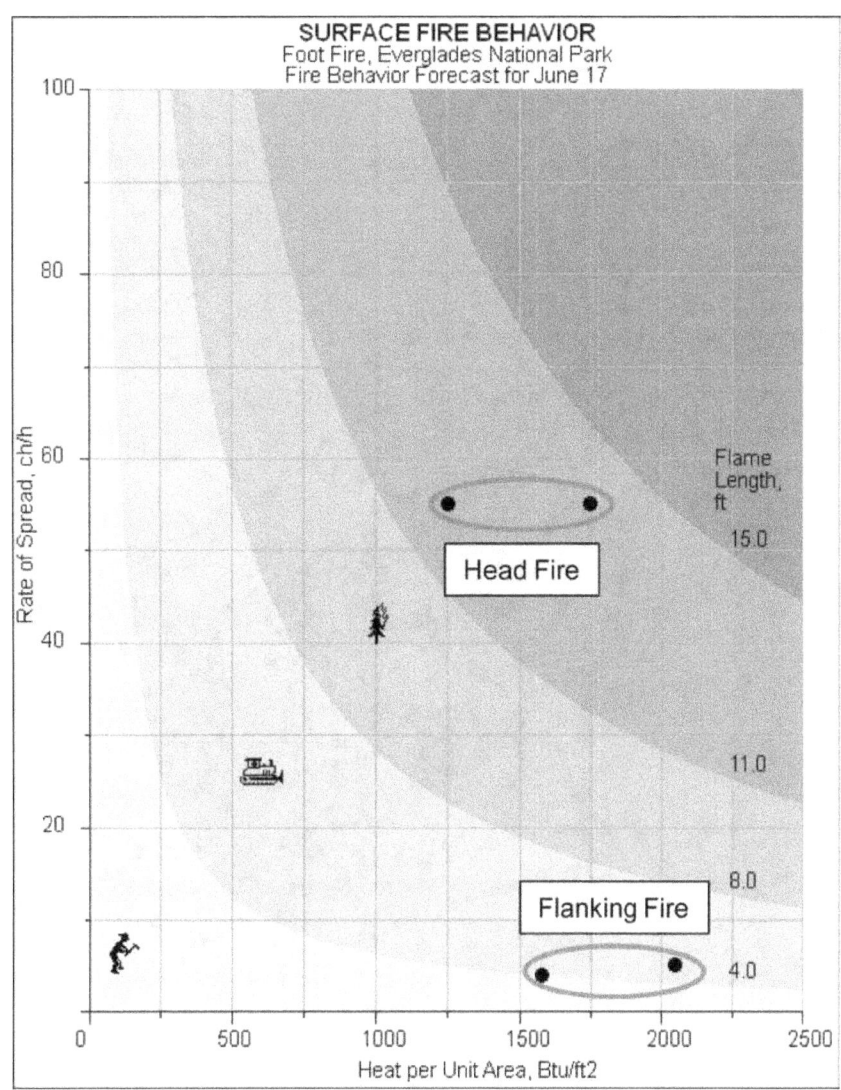

Figure 16—Fire characteristics chart illustrating expected fire behavior from the Fire Behavior Forecast in Figure 15.

The authors noted: "Calculation of fireline intensity for specific areas of this fire demonstrates that two different types of fire can have the same resistance to control: a fire spreading rapidly through fuels with low energy density, and a fire spreading more slowly but through fuel with higher energy densities."

Figure 17 shows the different fireline intensities within the Black Tiger Fire. Area labels are shown on the associated fire characteristics chart in Figure 18.

3 Program Operation_____

3.1 Overview

The Fire Characteristics Chart program is a stand-alone program that provides a means for plotting fire behavior values that are obtained elsewhere. BehavePlus or another program can be used to calculate values, or fire behavior values can be obtained from the field observations.

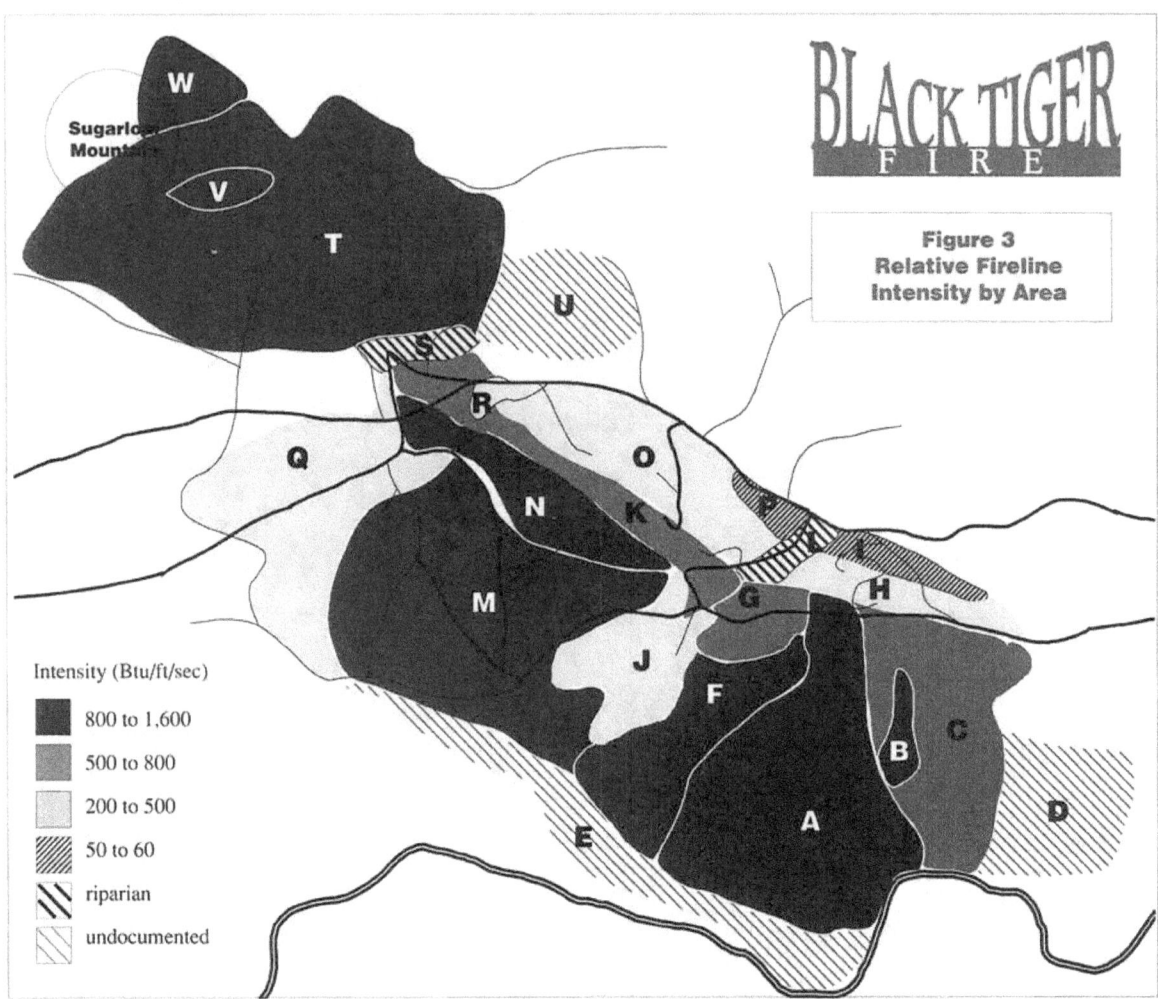

Figure 17—From NFPA (1990), Black Tiger Fire. Relative fireline intensity by area. These areas are referenced in Figure 18.

The charts are based on mathematical relationships among four variables: Rate of spread (ROS), heat per unit area (HPUA), flame length (FL), and fireline intensity (FLI). There are separate charts for surface and crown fire behavior because of the different relationship between fireline intensity and flame length for each (see Modeling Foundation section). A plotted point is defined by two values, either ROS and HPUA or ROS and FL. A toggle in the program lets you switch from one input option to the other, and values are typed directly into the worksheets.

Data and chart format settings can be saved for later use. The program opens with default settings, but you can open a saved file to use as a template. Chart default settings can be restored without deleting the data, and data can be deleted without altering chart settings.

The following are among many options for customizing the chart:

- Graph limits can be changed.
- Colors on the chart can be shades of red, rainbow colors, or shades of grey. Alternatively, flame length lines can be drawn without color or shading.
- Images can be added to the surface fire chart or left off. Custom images can be developed and used.
- Flame length values used to define curves can be changed.
- Units can be changed.
- Font type and size on the chart can be changed.
- Point icons, labels, and the legend can be changed.

Although the program offers many options for display, it certainly will not meet all needs. Additional labels can

USDA Forest Service Gen. Tech. Rep. RMRS-GTR-253. 2011

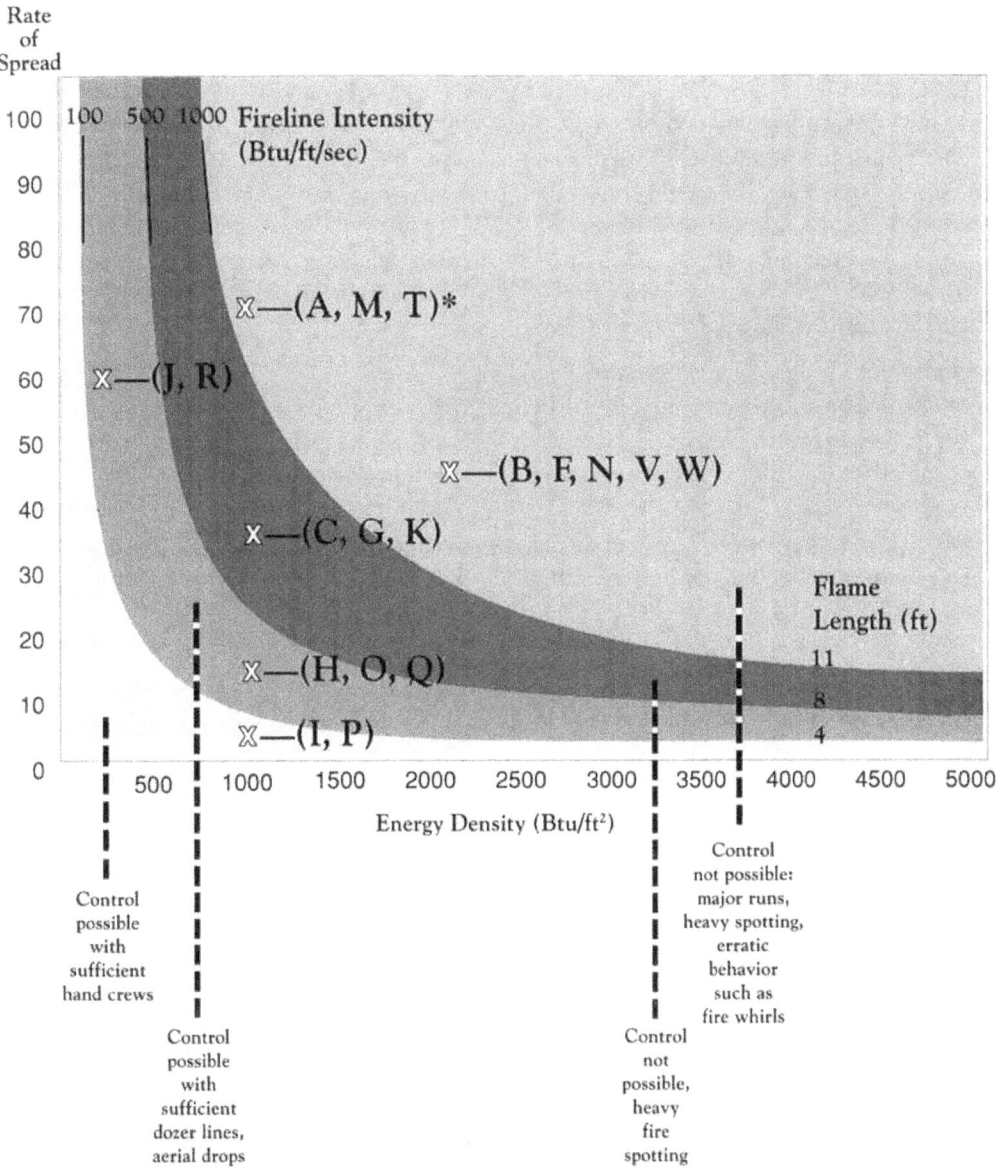

Figure 18—From NFPA (1990), Black Tiger Fire, fire characteristics chart showing the character of the fire for locations shown in Figure 17.

be added to a basic chart using other software, as was done for many of the Application section figures.

The following sections provide a detailed description of program operation. This document is included as the Help system for the program. Bookmarks help you find the appropriate section to answer your question.

3.1.1 Installation

The Fire Characteristics Chart installation program (**FireChart.msi**) can be downloaded from the BehavePlus website. Once you have saved the program, double-click on **FireChart.msi** to install the executable and associated files. The Fire Characteristics Chart operates on computers running Microsoft® Windows 2000, XP, Vista, or Windows 7. You will be prompted to save the program to the location of your choice. The program will default to the folder **C:/BehavePlus/FireChart**. You can save the program files anywhere on your computer by simply changing the location at the prompt. However, we recommend that you not save the program to the folder **C:/Program Files** since administrative privileges associated with this folder may affect program operation.

USDA Forest Service Gen. Tech. Rep. RMRS-GTR-253. 2011

21

3.1.2 Opening and Closing the Program

Each time you open the program, it opens the surface fire chart with default settings (Figure 19). You can then open a saved file with the settings that you prefer to use as a template. The command **File > Exit** allows the user to exit the program; however, any data and settings that are not saved will be lost. For more information on saving data and settings, see Section 3.4.1.

3.1.3 The Fire Characteristics Chart Window

The header shows the program name and version number. Beneath the header are three menu items: **File**, **Options**, and **Help** (described in Section 3.1.6). The left-hand side of the program window is the worksheet; the right-hand side is the chart (Figure 19). You change between the Surface Fire Behavior and Crown Fire Behavior worksheets by clicking on the appropriate tab.

3.1.4 Worksheet

The worksheet is the form in which data are entered. There are separate worksheets for surface and crown fire behavior, identified by separate tabs. Each worksheet contains three sections: Caption Lines, the Data Table, and Graph Definitions (Figure 20). The surface and crown fire behavior worksheets are similar, with differences in units selection. Also, the crown fire behavior worksheet does not offer images for curve labels.

3.1.5 Docking and Undocking the Worksheet

Increase graph size by removing the worksheet from the program window, clicking anywhere on the **Double click to dock/undock** menu bar (Figure 21). This option allows the user to move the worksheet to a different area on the computer monitor, thereby enlarging the graph. To re-attach the worksheet, simply double-click on it; it

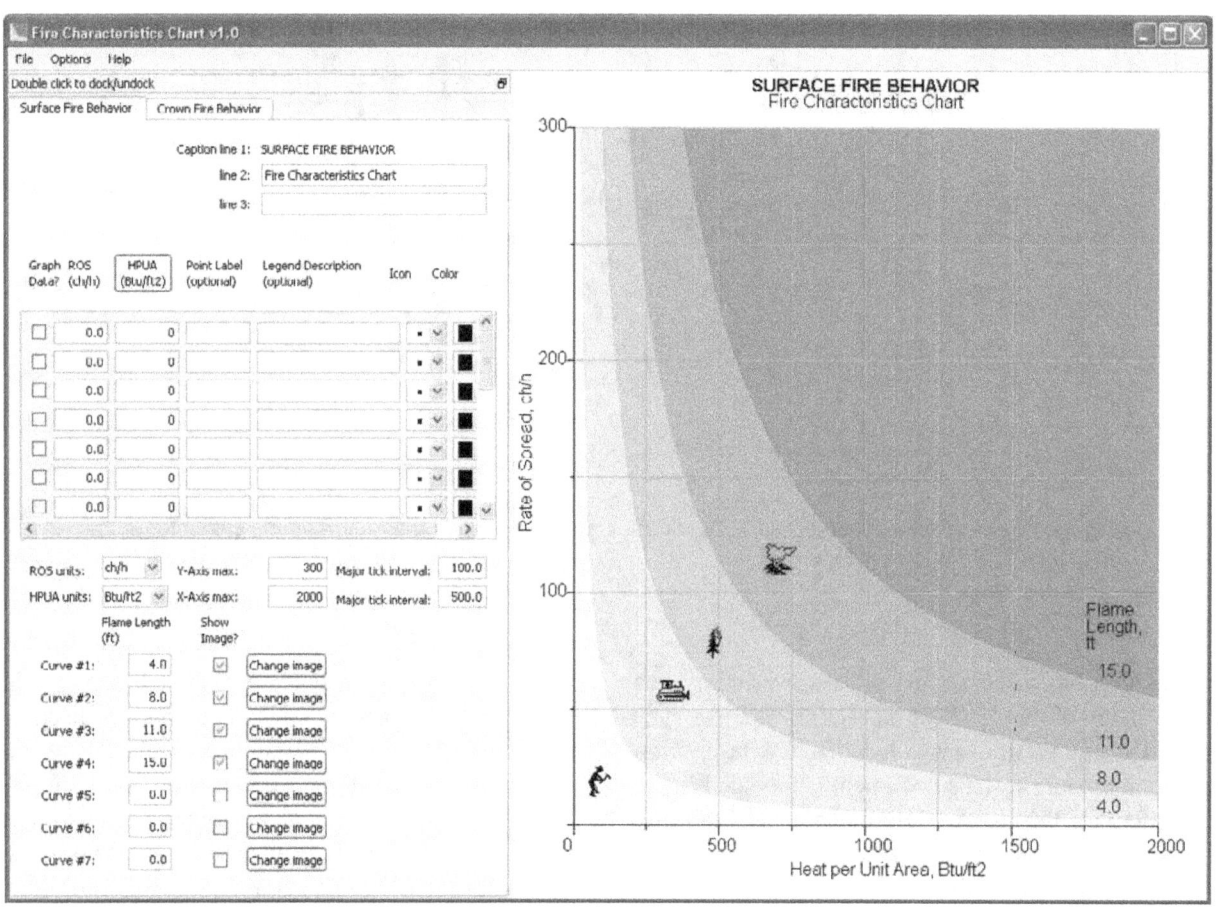

Figure 19—The Fire Characteristics Chart window contains both Surface Fire Behavior and Crown Fire Behavior worksheets (left-hand side) and a chart (right-hand side).

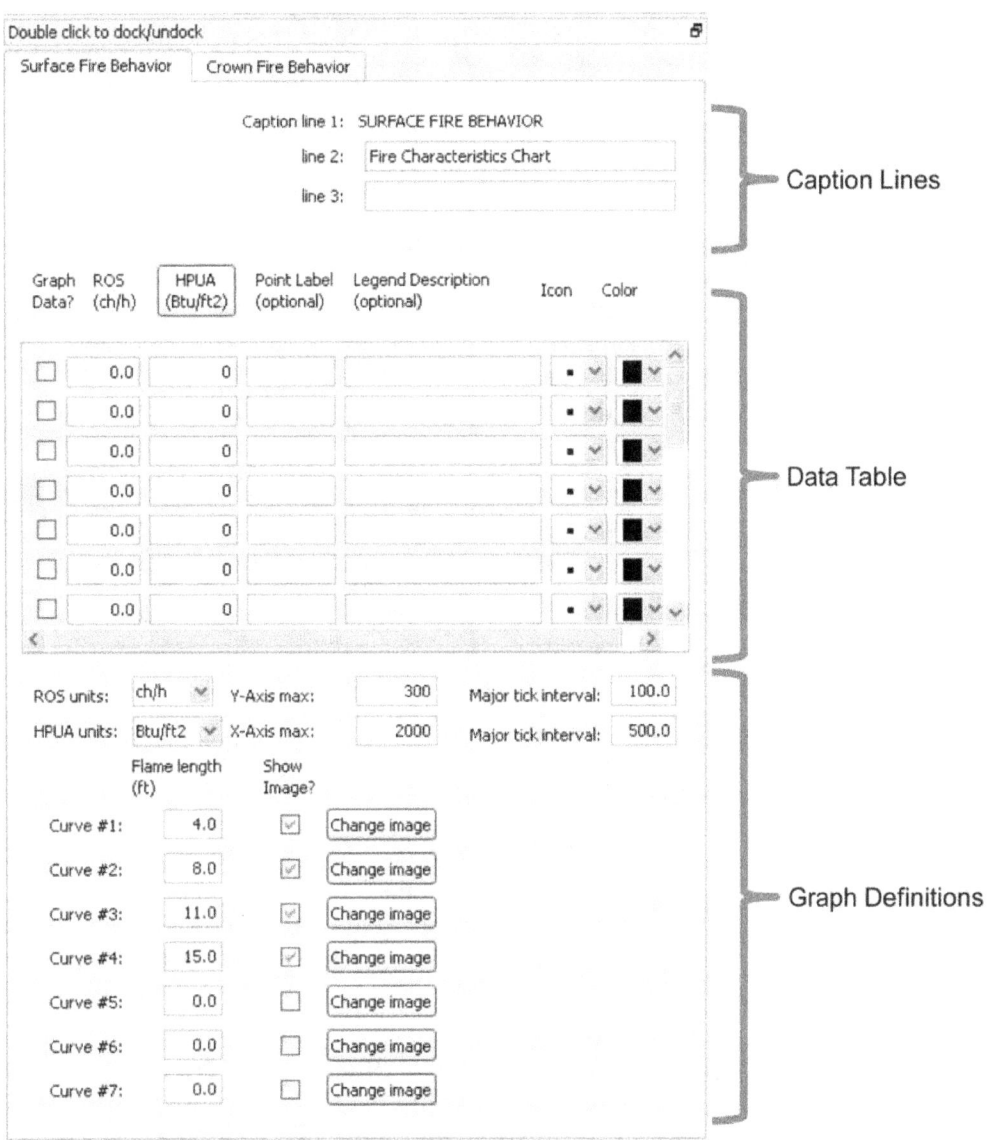

Figure 20—The Fire Characteristics Chart worksheet is divided into three sections: Caption Lines, Data Table, and Graph Definitions.

Figure 21—The worksheet can be removed from the graph by double-clicking anywhere on the Double click to dock/undock menu bar or on the icon circled in red. Double-click on the worksheet again to return it to the program window.

USDA Forest Service Gen. Tech. Rep. RMRS-GTR-253. 2011

23

will always attach to the left-hand side of the program window. If the worksheet is detached when the program is closed, the worksheet will return to the left-hand side of the program window when it is re-opened.

3.1.6 Menu Items

The main menu items are **File**, **Options**, and **Help**. These items will guide you to relevant operations within the Fire Characteristics Chart. **File** offers a means of opening, saving, and printing files (Figure 22). Files that have been previously saved can be accessed using the command **Open Fire Characteristics Chart data (.fcd) file**. The program is closed using the **File > Exit** command.

Files can be saved in three ways:

- All data and settings (**Save data and settings to .fcd file**)
- The chart itself (**Save image file...**)
- The worksheet, including all of the data (**Save data as HTML...**)

In addition, the program allows you to print just the chart (**Print Chart**) or the entire window, including both the worksheet and the chart (**Print Window**). Printing options can be modified using the **Page setup...** command.

The **Options** menu (Figure 23) provides access to the **Graph options...**, where you can modify chart settings. To restore the chart to the program default settings without deleting data, select **Restore settings to default...**. To clear the worksheet and return worksheet settings to default without changing the chart, choose **Clear data...**. To clear everything, select both options or exit the program and re-open it.

The **Help** menu (Figure 24) gives information about the program and links to this report.

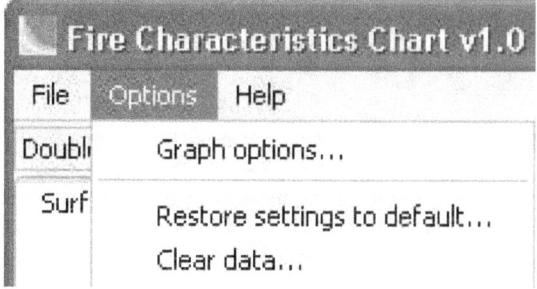

Figure 23—The Options menu provides access to graph options and settings.

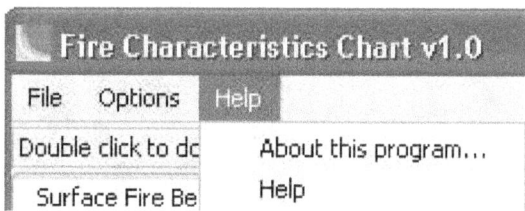

Figure 24—The Help menu gives information about the program and opens this report.

3.2 Chart Format

Options for defining chart format are found on the Graph Definitions portion of the worksheet (Figure 20) and under **Options > Graph options...** (Figure 25). In the worksheet's Graph Definitions section, you can select data units, the graph scale, and tick mark intervals, as well as define flame length curves. **Graph options...** allows you to show/hide gridlines, choose colors, or use and format the legend. Changes affect *only* the graph in the active tab (Surface Fire Behavior or Crown Fire Behavior). All of the chart format options described in this section are reset to default settings for the active tab using **Options > Restore settings to default...**.

3.2.1 Units

Both English and metric units are available and are set in the Graph Definitions section of both worksheets using drop-down menus beside **ROS units** and **HPUA units**. Surface fire English units are: ROS—ch/h, ft/min, or mi/h; HPUA—Btu/ft^2; and FL—feet. Metric units are: ROS—km/h, m/s, or m/min; HPUA—kJ/m^2; and FL—meters.

There are fewer unit selections for the Crown Fire Behavior worksheet, but the worksheet behaves the same way. Crown fire ROS is expressed as either mi/h or km/h; HPUA is either Btu/ft^2 or kJ/m^2; and FL is either feet or meters.

Figure 22—The File menu offers a means of opening, saving, and printing files.

Open Fire Characteristics Chart data (.fcd) file	Ctrl+O
Save data and settings to .fcd file	Ctrl+S
Save image file...	Ctrl+I
Save data as HTML...	
Page setup...	
Print Chart	Ctrl+P
Print Window	
Exit	Ctrl+X

24

USDA Forest Service Gen. Tech. Rep. RMRS-GTR-253. 2011

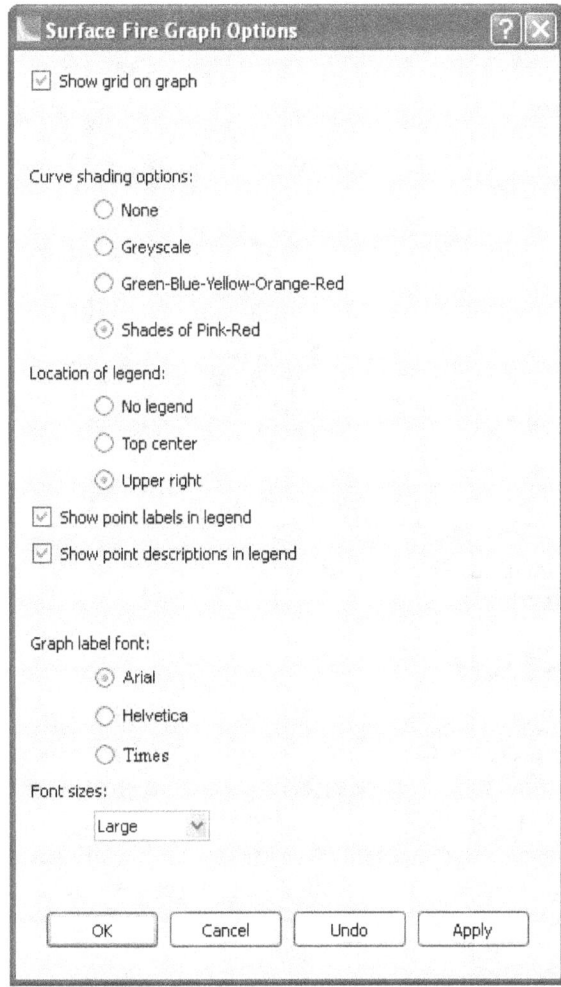

Figure 25—The Graph Options window controls the look of the chart.

(ROS) is 500 ch/h. The upper limit for the Crown Fire Behavior Y-Axis is 20 mi/h. If you type in a larger value, the program will automatically reset it to the upper limit. Similarly, the X-Axis (HPUA) maximum can be changed. The upper limit for the Surface Fire Behavior X-Axis is 5000 Btu/ft^2. The upper limit for the Crown Fire Behavior X-Axis is 10,000 Btu/ft^2.

The program will automatically estimate a tick mark interval, which, in most cases, is appropriate. The tick mark intervals can be changed by typing a new tick mark interval in the **Major tick interval** box on the worksheet. If you reset the graph scale, the program will estimate a new tick mark interval. Gridlines can be removed by unchecking the **Show grid on graph** box in the **Graph Options** menu (Section 3.2.6).

3.2.3 Flame Length Curves

As many as seven flame length curves are available on both the Surface and Crown Fire Behavior charts. Each curve can be denoted by a change in color on the graph. The colorway can be changed using the **Curve shading options** in the **Graph Options** menu. Values for flame length curves must appear sequentially from smallest to largest for the program to draw curves correctly. If they are entered in a different order, the program will sort them automatically. Curves with a flame length of zero will be moved to the end of the list automatically and will not appear on the graph. A change from English to metric units may result in values that need to be changed to more reasonable, rounded values.

The default Surface Fire Behavior chart setup contains four curves with FL of 4, 8, 11, and 15 ft. These curves can be interpreted as ranging from fires that can easily be controlled by hand crews, to fires for which tractors or bulldozers are required, to fires on which control efforts at the head of the fire will be ineffective (Table 1; Andrews and Rothermel 1982). The images provide a rough graphical indication of the intensity of the fire (Section 3.2.4). Icons are associated with the curve number, not the flame length value, and it is your responsibility to ensure that the icons are correct when modifying flame length curve values.

The default Crown Fire Behavior chart setup contains seven curves with FL values of 20, 50, 100, 150, 200, 250, and 300 ft. Icons are not available for the crown fire chart.

3.2.4 Flame Length Images

Images related to the Surface Fire Behavior worksheet flame length curves are located in a folder titled **ChartImages** in the program folder (Figure 26) and can

When the user switches from English to metric units (or vice versa), the graph updates automatically, converting all values for ROS, HPUA, and FL to metric values. This switch also applies to the maximum values on the graph. If the user changes units within a given measurement system, the units and settings of the other axis and the curves may or may not change, depending upon the units selected. For example, changing from ch/h to ft/min will not change the maximum Y-Axis value, while changing from ch/h to mi/h will change it.

3.2.2 Graph Scale and Tick Marks

Graph scales are modified by setting the maximum values; minimum values are always zero. The Y-Axis represents the ROS, and the maximum value can be changed by typing a number into the **Y-Axis** max box. The upper limit for the Surface Fire Behavior Y-Axis

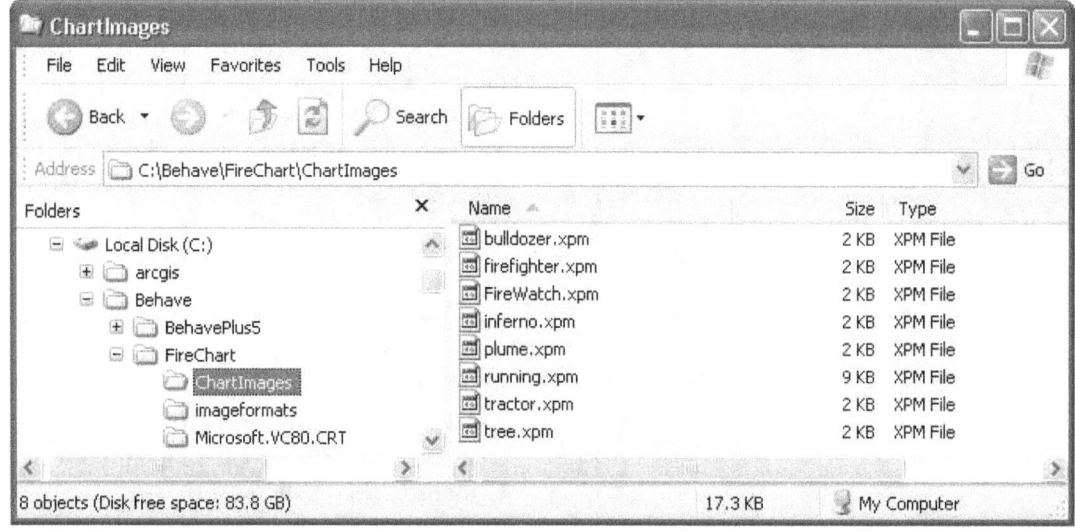

Figure 26—Flame length curve images are stored in the ChartImages folder.

be shown by placing a checkmark in the **Show Image?** box next to the image. The images can be changed by using the **Change image** button next to each curve. We have created a series of default images for the surface fire behavior curves (Table 1), and we have included two additional images of a standing firefighter carrying a shovel (representing, perhaps, FL<1 ft) and of a tractor.

You can easily develop your own images. The images used in this program are black and white X Pixmap files. Custom images can be created using any graphics software. Your image should be saved in bitmap (.bmp) format and then converted to X Pixmap (.xpm) files using a converter program. We recommend that you store your images in the ChartImages folder located in the program folder. However, if you have saved a custom image elsewhere, you can easily navigate to it.

3.2.5 Graph Options

Many of the graph's appearance settings are made using the **Options > Graph options...** window (Figure 25). Gridlines can be added to the graph, and changes can be made to curve shading, the legend, and graph fonts. Clicking on the **Apply** button will apply your changes to the graph without closing the **Graph Options** window. You can undo applied changes using the **Undo** button. **Cancel** will close the window without making any changes that have not yet been applied. Click on **OK** to apply changes *and* close the **Graph Options** window. If a file is opened that contains different graph options than those currently selected, the settings associated with the file will override the current graph options. Files can be saved and used as templates (3.4.1).

3.2.6 Grid

Gridlines for both the X- and Y-Axes are visible by default. They can be removed (turned off) by removing the checkmark next to **Show grid on graph** in the **Graph Options** window (Figure 25). The tick mark interval is specified on the worksheet. This interval will be calculated automatically, but it can easily be changed (Section 3.2.2).

3.2.7 Graph Color

Select the graph's colorway by selecting the **FL curve shading options** (Figure 25). These options include: **None** (black lines on a white background), **Greyscale, Green-Blue-Yellow-Orange-Red,** or **Shades of Pink-Red** (default). Colors are associated with curve numbers, not flame length values.

3.2.8 Legend

A legend is available for identifying points on the graph. Within the legend, there are options to show point labels and/or the legend description. This may be helpful when the same point icon is used for more than one point (Sections 3.3.5 and 3.3.6).

The placement and format of the legend can be changed in **Options > Graph Options....** The legend is placed inside the graph, either at the center (**Top center**) or in the upper right-hand corner (**Upper right**). You can also remove the legend by selecting **No legend**. At times, the legend may hide plotted data points. If this is a problem, you can change the axis scales to reveal the data point, remove the legend, or add a legend later using other software.

3.2.9 Font

Graph fonts can be changed using **Options > Graph Options > Graph label font**. There are three available fonts: **Arial**, **Helvetica**, and **Times New Roman**, which can be selected using radio dial buttons (Figure 25). Font size may be an issue in crowded graphs, so there are five options that range from **Very Small** to **Very Large**, which can be selected using a drop-down menu. The default font is **Arial**, and the default font size is **Large**. Changes to the graph font will affect all text on the graph, including axis labels, point labels, and the legend.

3.2.10 Restore Settings to Default

To start over when customizing the graph format, select **Options > Restore settings to default…** (Figure 27). This action will revert to the default graph settings on the active tab for both the graph definition portion of

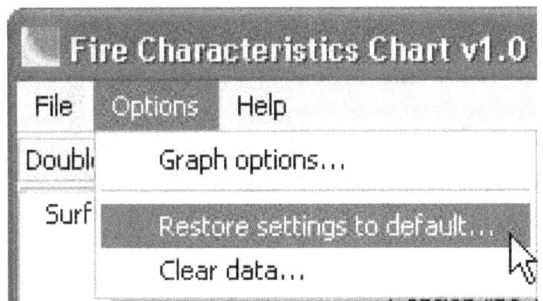

Figure 27—Selecting **Options > Restore settings to default…** will set the graph options to the default values.

the worksheet (Figure 20) and the **Options > Graph options…** window (Figure 25). Data are not deleted. However, if metric units are used, the data will be converted to the default English units (Section 3.2.1).

3.3 Entering Data

In the following sections, we describe worksheet data entry (Figure 28). This includes not just the data values but all entries on the worksheet. All entries described in this section are cleared for the active tab using **Options > Clear data**. Clearing the data does not change the chart settings (Section 3.2.10).

3.3.1 Caption Lines

As many as three **Caption lines** can be added to the graph for clarity (Figure 20). **Caption line 1** is automatically generated to properly identify the graph as **SURFACE FIRE BEHAVIOR** or **CROWN FIRE BEHAVIOR**. The second and third caption lines are optional and can be customized to provide more detailed information about the graph. For example, **Caption line 2** could be "Burn Plan X" or the name of the fire. **Caption line 3** may provide more specific information about the project, such as the date the worksheet was created or the date of the fire. Caption lines are limited to 50 characters.

3.3.2 Data Points

Before entering any data values, it is important to decide whether you will be entering ROS and HPUA or ROS and FL. Use the toggle button to ensure the correct variable (HPUA or FL) is active. Make certain that the

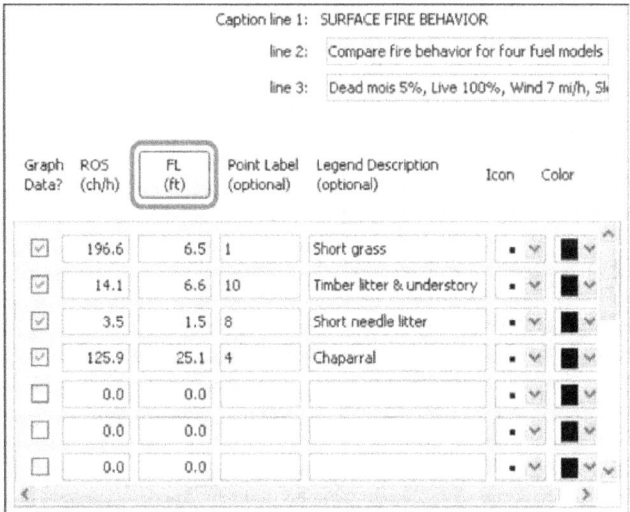

Figure 28—The third column of the Data Table of the worksheet toggles between (a) Heat per Unit Area, HPUA, and (b) Flame Length, FL.

units in the Graph Definitions section of the worksheet (Figure 20) are correctly set. Remember, a change in units after data entry will change data values.

The ROS is entered in column 2, while HPUA and FL share the third column. Toggling on the box at the top of column 3 will switch between the two variables. Values for ROS and either HPUA *or* FL must be entered. The other term will be calculated as described in the Modeling Foundation section. The program will *not* check for illogical values for ROS, HPUA, or FL. It is your responsibility to ensure that the values entered on the graph make sense.

If you enter a value for either HPUA or FL and toggle back and forth between the two variables several times, the values may "drift" because of round-off issues in the calculations. However, entering values once and toggling to the other variable should not cause a problem. Zero is a valid input for all three variables and will appear on the graph and in the legend if the **Graph Data**? box is checked (Section 3.3.3). Entering values outside the plot scale limits (Section 3.2.2) is possible, but the values will not appear on the graph. If a point label or legend description has been entered for that value, however, the point will appear in the legend.

3.3.3 Graph Data

If the box in the **Graph Data**? column is checked, a point corresponding to the data in that row will be plotted on the graph *and* create a line in the legend. If the **Graph Data**? box is not checked, the data are ignored. However, these data will be saved in both Fire Characteristics Chart data files (Section 3.4.1) and HTML files (Section 3.4.4).

3.3.4 Point Icons

The icon and color for the plotted point are selected from drop-down menus for **Icon** and **Color**. There are 10 possible icons in column 6 that that can be used to distinguish among data points and 10 possible colors to select in column 7 (Figure 29).

3.3.5 Point Label

Up to six characters can be entered in the **Point Label** column to label a point on the chart. If you leave it blank, the point will appear on the graph, but there will be no label marking the point, and the point will not appear in the legend unless there is a **Legend Description**. By default, the label will appear both on the graph and in the legend. The user can change the legend settings if desired (Section 3.2.8). At times, point labels may appear above the chart, interfering with the chart title. To fix this, simply increase the Y-Axis maximum value.

3.3.6 Legend Description

A longer description can be entered for each point in the optional **Legend Description** column, providing more information for the legend (Figure 30). By default, it appears at the end of the legend, although legend settings can be changed if desired (Section 3.2.8). The **Legend Description** can be 35 characters in length.

3.3.7 Clear Data

The menu item **Options > Clear data** clears everything in the worksheet data table (Figures 20 and 31), including the data values, point labels, legend description, and icon/color selections. It will not, however, affect the graph settings (Section 3.2.10). This command applies only to data in the current tab.

3.4 Saved Files

The program opens with the default graph settings and a blank worksheet. Data and graph format settings can be saved to a file for later use. Data values and the graph can be saved separately for documentation purposes. The default location for saving all files is the program folder, but files can be saved in any location on your computer.

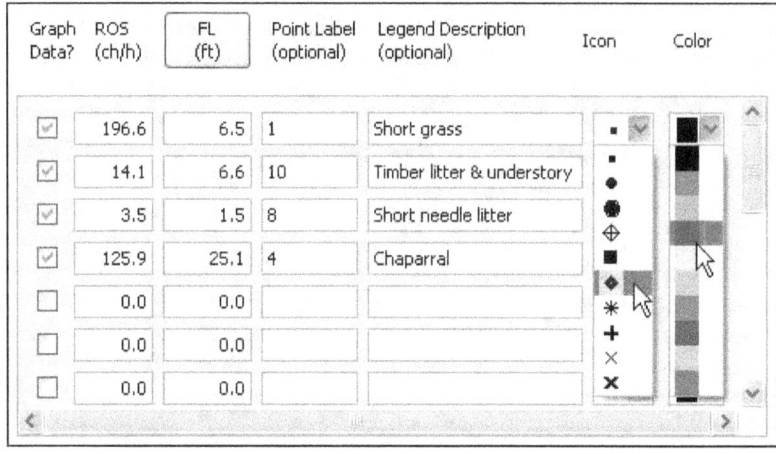

Figure 29—There are 10 possible point icons and colors for use in the Fire Characteristics Chart program.

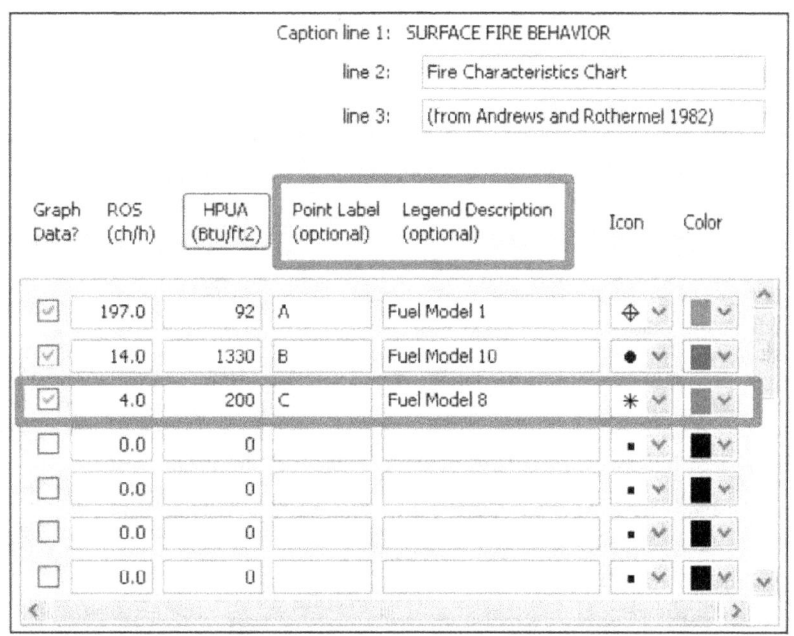

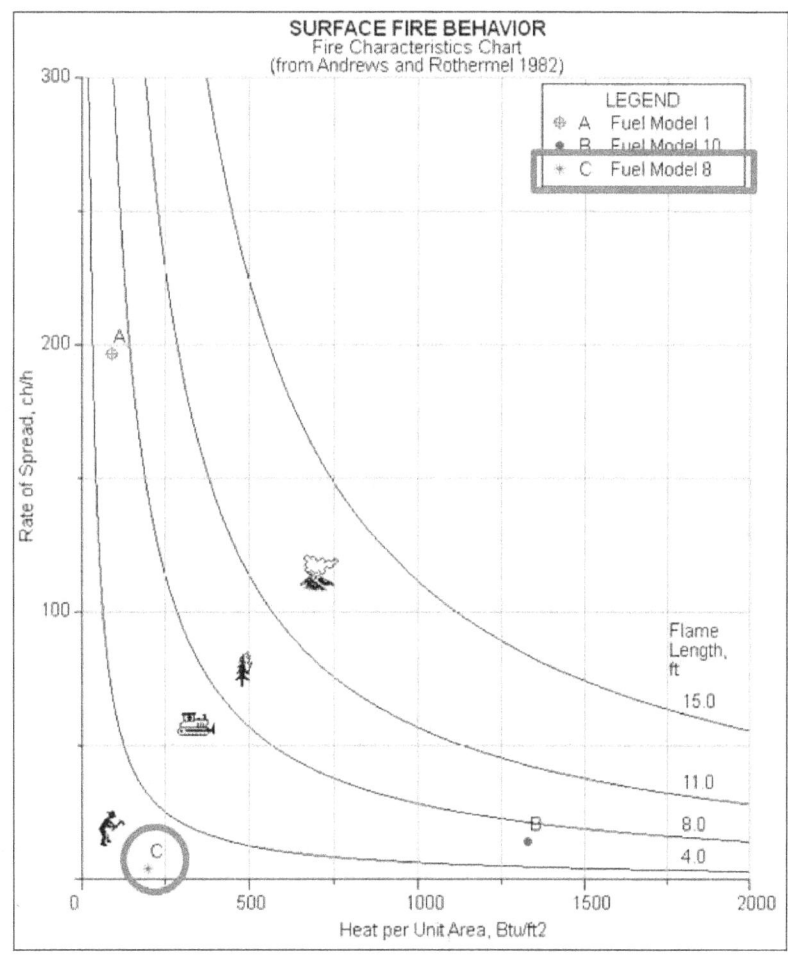

Figure 30—The **Point Label** and **Legend Description** from the data table are used to identify the points in the graph and/or the legend.

USDA Forest Service Gen. Tech. Rep. RMRS-GTR-253. 2011

29

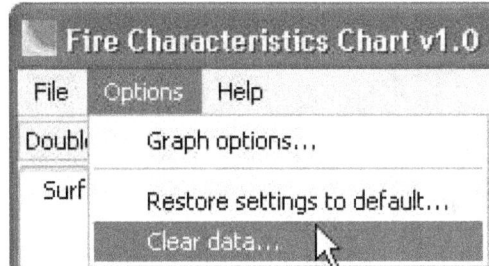

Figure 31—Selecting **Options > Clear data...** will delete all data in the active worksheet.

3.4.1 Saving a Fire Characteristics Chart File

Data and settings can be saved to a Fire Characteristics Chart data file (.fcd) by selecting **File > Save data and settings to .fcd file** (Figure 22). These files contain *both* data values and graph settings for a given chart and can only be used within the Fire Characteristics Chart program. You may wish to clear the data and save the file as a template of personal preferences to use in place of default settings. Data and settings are saved only for the active worksheet; if there are data in both tabs, they must be saved separately.

3.4.2 Opening a Fire Characteristics Chart File

The **File > Open Fire Characteristics Chart data (.fcd) file** command is used to open a Fire Characteristics Chart file that was previously saved. The Surface Fire Behavior and Crown Fire Behavior worksheets operate independently, but the program will ensure the correct tab is active when a file is opened.

3.4.3 Save Image File

Graphs can be saved as images in the following formats: JPEG (.jpg), Windows bitmap (.bmp), and Portable Network Graphics (.png). Once the graph is complete, click on **File > Save image file...**, select the desired location and file format, and save the graph. The resulting image can be easily used in documentation or can be edited using other software.

3.4.4 Saving Data as HTML

When you print a chart or save it as an image, you should document the information needed to reproduce it, including data values represented on the chart. To assist in documentation, the worksheet can be exported as an HTML file that contains all of the data points, including those that do not appear on the screen (Figure 32). This file can be included in reports with the chart so that others can recreate your chart if desired.

3.5 Printing

The Fire Characteristics Chart can be printed using the **File > Print** command (Figure 22). The program will send the graph to the selected printer. Only the graph can be printed, not the worksheet. It is a good idea to use caption lines (Section 3.3.1) to clearly describe the graph.

Use the **File > Page setup...** command to modify print settings for the program (Figure 33). Select the paper size, source, orientation (either Portrait or Landscape), and

Figure 32—A worksheet can be saved as an HTML file for documenting the data used in creating the fire characteristics chart.

printer margins to customize print settings. The default printer margins are set by your printer. The printer can be identified (**File > Page Setup > Printer...**) before clicking **OK** to save the selections. Selecting **Cancel** will cancel the current selections and return to the main program. Printer settings are only valid for the current session of the Fire Characteristics Chart.

3.6 Adding Custom Labels

The Fire Characteristics Chart program will not meet all user needs. In particular, users may want to emphasize certain portions of the graph (e.g., Figure 30) by adding custom labels. To add custom labels, you should make a screen capture of the chart or save it as an image file and use other software to add additional lines, circles, or text to the graph.

3.7 Help

The Help button on the Menu Bar (**Help > About this program...**) provides information about the program, including the version number (Figure 34) and contact information for the developers.

Clicking on **Help > Help** opens this document. You can navigate to the section of interest using the bookmarks.

4 Modeling Foundation

In this section, we describe the relationship among the variables used to produce the fire characteristics charts described in this paper. A person whose application is not satisfied by the options offered in our program can use these equations to develop their own chart. We do not provide complete details of the calculation of values plotted on the chart (ROS, HPUA, FL, FLI) since points plotted on the chart are calculated elsewhere.

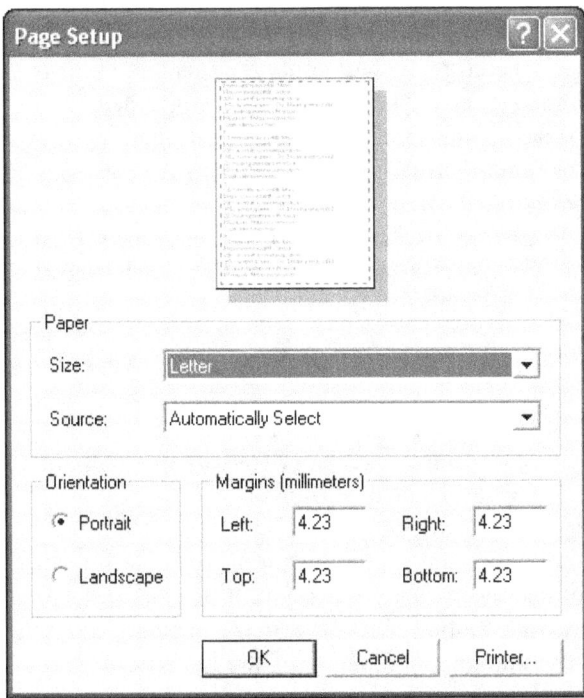

Figure 33—The Page Setup option window allows the user to define page margins and orientation for the current session.

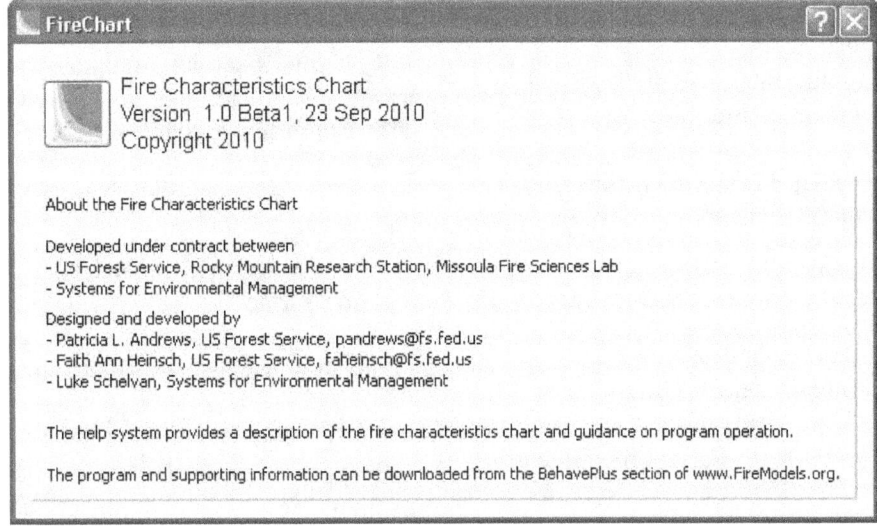

Figure 34—Information about this program can be found in the **Help > About this program...** box.

4.1 Surface Fire Behavior

The mathematical basis for the surface fire characteristics chart includes Rothermel's (1972) surface fire spread model, Byram's (1959) fireline intensity and flame length models, Anderson's (1969) residence time model, and the linkages among them. These models address only the flaming front of the surface fire, which is influenced primarily by fine fuels. The surface fire model describes fire spreading through fuels that include litter, grass, brush, and other dead and live vegetation within about 6 ft of the ground. It does not include organic ground fuel (duff) or large fuel that burns after the flaming front has passed.

Surface fire rate of spread is calculated using Rothermel's model from a description of the fuel (often a fuel model), fuel moisture, wind speed, and slope. Heat per unit area is available from intermediate calculations in the spread model. Byram's fireline intensity is calculated from rate of spread and heat per unit area, forming the basis for the fire characteristics chart.

$$I_B = H_A R \qquad (1)$$

where

I_B = Byram's fireline intensity (Btu/ft/s),
H_A = heat per unit area (Btu/ ft^2), and
R = rate of spread (ft/s).

Changing units to match those used for the fire characteristic charts in Andrews and Rothermel (1982) and rearranging equation (1) to plot the curves for specified values of fireline intensity gives:

$$R = 55 \, I_B / H_A \qquad (2)$$

where

R = rate of spread (ch/h),
I_B = Byram's fireline intensity (Btu/ft/s), and
H_A = heat per unit area (Btu/ ft^2).

Flame length is calculated from fireline intensity, according to Byram's (1959) equation.

$$F_B = 0.45 \, I_B{}^{0.46} \qquad (3)$$

where

F_B = Byram's flame length (ft) and
I_B = Byram's fireline intensity (Btu/ft/s).

Byram (1959) presented his model for fireline intensity as:

$$I_B = H w \, R \qquad (4)$$

where

I_B = Byram's fireline intensity (Btu/ft/s),
H = heat yield (Btu/lb of fuel),
w = weight of the available fuel (lb/ft^2), and
R = rate of spread (ft/s).

Heat per unit area (H_A) is used to estimate Hw, leading to equation (1). Heat per unit area is the heat energy release per unit area within the flaming front. "Available fuel," therefore, includes only the fuel that burns in the flaming front and not the total fuel consumed.

Heat per unit area is derived from Rothermel's model. Reaction intensity is the rate of energy release per unit area within the flaming front and is an intermediate value in Rothermel's calculation of rate of spread. Heat per unit area is reaction intensity multiplied by the flame residence time, such that

$$H_A = I_R \, t_r \qquad (5)$$

where

H_A = heat per unit area (Btu/ft^2),
I_R = reaction intensity (Btu/ft^2/min), and
t_r = residence time (min).

Residence time is the length of time that it takes the fire front to pass a given point. It does not include the indefinite trailing edge of the fire. Anderson (1969) found that a good approximation of the flaming time of fuel particles burning in a uniform fuel array can be calculated from fuel particle size.

$$t_r = 8 \, d \qquad (6)$$

where

t_r = residence time (min) and
d = fuel particle diameter (inches).

Rothermel's surface fire spread model uses surface-area-to-volume ratio as a measure of fuel particle size. The relationship to diameter is:

$$d = 48 / \sigma \qquad (7)$$

where

d = fuel particle diameter (inches) and
σ = surface-area-to-volume ratio (inches^2/inches^3).

Substituting equation (7) into equation (6) gives:

$$t_r = 384 / \sigma \qquad (8)$$

Heat per unit area can then be calculated from factors available in the calculation of rate of spread using Rothermel's (1972) model.

$$H_A = 384 \, I_R / \sigma \qquad (9)$$

4.2 Crown Fire Behavior

Rothermel (1991) provided methods for predicting the spread rate, intensity, and size of crown fires. He developed a model for crown fire rate of spread based on his surface fire spread model (Rothermel 1972). He used Byram's (1959) model for fireline intensity, Thomas' (1963) model for flame length, and Albini's (1976a) burnout model in estimating surface heat per unit area. He presented a crown fire characteristics chart to display observed and modeled crown fire behavior.

Byram's model for fireline intensity, stated in terms of heat per unit area and rate of spread, is used as the basis for the crown fire characteristics chart as well as for the surface fire chart (equation 1).

Rothermel (1991) presented a simple model for crown fire rate of spread. He developed a correlation between observed crown fire rate of spread and a calculated value using his surface fire spread model. Observed crown fire spread rate was determined using spread distance and elapsed time for seven crown fires. The length of time for the crown fire runs in Rothermel's study ranged from 0.83 to 5 hours, over which time conditions certainly varied significantly, with fire spread being strongly influenced by spotting.

The model for average crown fire spread rate is simply 3.34 times the spread rate calculated for a surface fire in fuel model 10 with a midflame wind speed equal to 0.4 of the 20-ft wind speed. Crown fire spread rate is calculated in BehavePlus from 20-ft wind speed and the moisture content of the dead and live surface fuels (the same moisture values used in the surface fire spread model). The crown fire spread rate model does not include a description of either the surface or the crown fuel.

While Byram's flame length model is used for surface fire (equation 3), it underpredicts the flame length of crown fires. Rothermel (1991) used Thomas' (1963) model because it produces flame lengths that "appear to be reasonable except at low intensity; no exact values for such a phenomenon can be fixed, but the numbers serve as useful guides to the intensity of the fire."

Crown fire flame length is calculated from fireline intensity, according to Thomas (1963), as:

$$F_T = 0.2\, I_B^{2/3} \qquad (10)$$

where
F_T = Thomas' flame length (ft) and
I_B = Byram's fireline intensity (Btu/ft/s).

Calculation of heat per unit area for crown fire requires estimation of the proportion of the fuel contributing to the development of the convection column. This includes both the surface fuel and canopy (overstory) fuel loads.

Crown fire heat per unit area is the sum of surface fire heat per unit area and canopy heat per unit area.

$$H_{A,crown} = H_{A,surface} + H_{A,canopy} \qquad (11)$$

where
$H_{A,crown}$ = heat per unit area of the crown fire,
$H_{A,surface}$ = heat per unit area contributed by the surface fuel, and
$H_{A,canopy}$ = heat per unit area contributed by the overstory canopy.

Surface fire heat per unit area can be calculated in BehavePlus using Rothermel's surface fire model, as described in Section 4.1, based on the fine fuels that carry the fire at the fire front. There is, however, an important contribution to fire intensity by accumulations of larger sizes of dead and downed fuel. Rothermel (1991) used Albini's (1976a) burnout model to estimate an alternate value for several of the standard fuel models, including two with additional heavy fuel. BehavePlus allows user-specified values for surface heat per unit area, which can be selected from those calculated by Rothermel (Table 4).

Rothermel assumed the contribution of canopy fuel to be the total energy release to be produced by the consumption of the conifer needles, assuming heat from the needles is 8000 Btu/lb (18,622 kJ/kg) of dry needles. The canopy contribution is:

$$H_{A,canopy} = Hw \qquad (12)$$

where
$H_{A,canopy}$ = heat per unit area of the canopy fuel (Btu/ft^2),
H = heat content (Btu/lb), and
w = crown load (lb/ft^2).

In BehavePlus, crown load is estimated by multiplying canopy bulk density by the difference between canopy height and canopy base height.

Table 4—Surface heat per unit area values calculated using Albini's burnout model (from Rothermel 1991).

Fuel model	Additional 1000-h fuel, tons/ac	Heat per unit area, Btu/ft^2
8		580
2		760
9		1050
9	30	1325
10		1325
10	30	1570
12		3430

4.3 Surface and Crown Fire Flame Length and Fireline Intensity

While both the surface and crown fire characteristics charts are based on the relationship of fireline intensity to rate of spread and heat per unit area, they use different models to calculate flame length from fireline intensity. Figure 35 shows a plot of Byram's flame length (equation 3, used for surface fire) and Thomas' flame length (equation 10, used for crown fire) as a function of fireline intensity. Note the significant difference.

A fire characteristics chart with curves based on fireline intensity and that is labeled with surface and crown fire flame lengths illustrates the issue of misinterpretation of the chart (Figure 36). A comparison of the surface and crown fire charts with the same flame length curves shows the difference between the flame length models (Figure 37).

Table 5 shows fireline intensity associated with selected surface flame length based on Byram (1959) for English and metric units. Similarly, Table 6 shows the relationship between crown fire flame length and fireline intensity based on Thomas (1963). Note that surface fire flame length of 20 ft is associated with fireline intensity of 3821 Btu/ft/s, while a crown fire flame length of 20 ft is associated with fireline intensity of 1000 Btu/ft/s. Given that the curves on the fire characteristics charts produced by our program are labeled with flame length, Tables 5 and 6 can be used as quick references for conversion to fireline intensity.

4.4 Other Forms of the Fire Characteristics Chart

In this report, we described surface and crown fire characteristics charts along with the mathematical relationships that form the basis for these charts. In this section, we provide a brief review of other forms of the fire characteristics chart. Each version of the chart depends on mathematical relationships among the modeled variables and its intended use.

Rothermel and Anderson (1966) presented results of laboratory experiments that led to development of the Rothermel (1972) surface fire spread model. They plotted data on what they called a fire characteristics chart, which related rate of spread and equivalent unit energy release rate, later called reaction intensity.

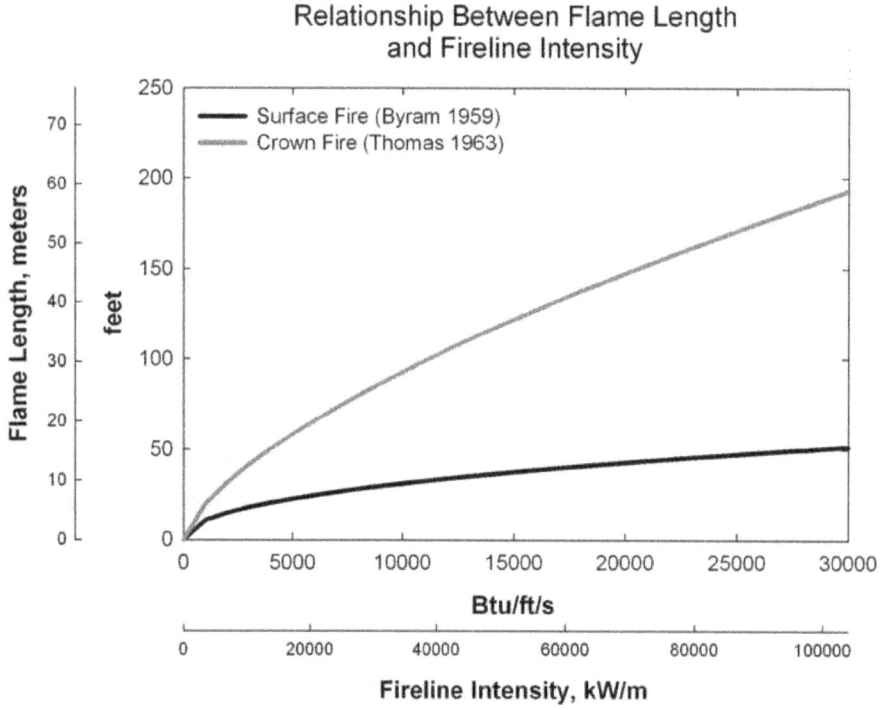

Figure 35—Flame length as a function of fireline intensity using Byram (1959) for surface fire and Thomas (1963) for crown fire.

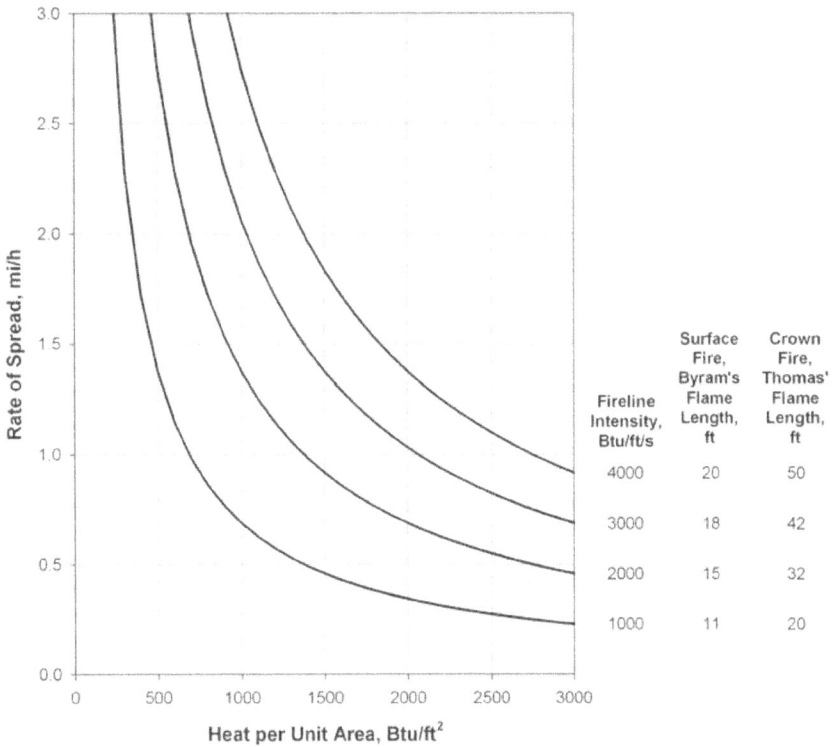

Figure 36—Fire characteristics chart with fireline intensity curves. The associated surface and crown fire flame lengths are given for each curve. To avoid potential misinterpretation, we do not offer this option in our program.

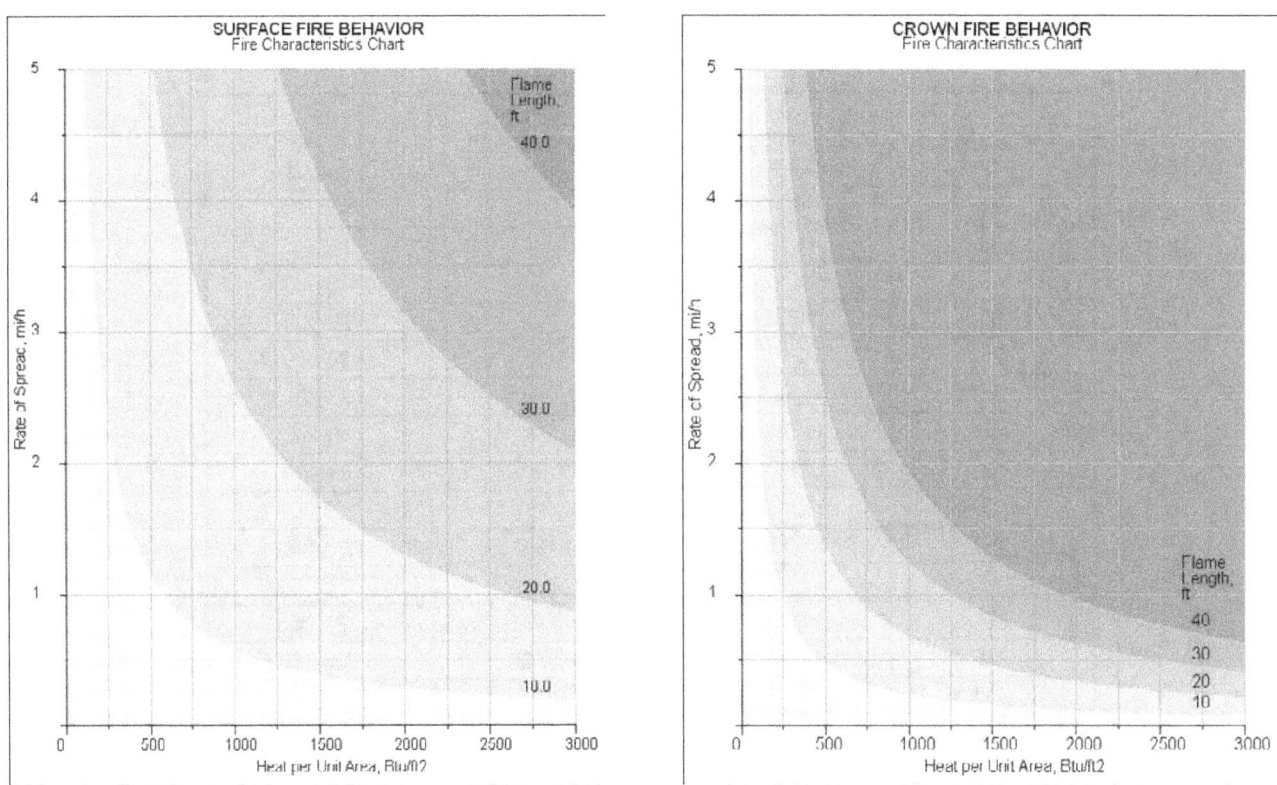

Figure 37—Comparison of the surface and crown fire characteristics charts with the same flame length curves. The difference is due to the difference in flame length equations.

Table 5—Relationship between selected values of surface fire flame length (Byram 1959) and fireline intensity for English and metric units.

Surface flame length, ft	Fireline intensity, Btu/ft/s	Surface flame length, m	Fireline intensity, kJ/m/s
1	6	0.5	1
2	26	1.0	6
3	62	1.5	14
4	116	2.0	26
5	188	2.5	42
6	279	3.0	62
7	390	3.5	86
8	521	4.0	116
9	673	4.5	149
10	847	5.0	188
11	1042	5.5	231
13	1498	6.0	279
15	2045		
20	3821		

Table 6—Relationship between selected values of crown fire flame length (Thomas 1963) and fireline intensity for English and metric units. (FLI values are rounded.)

Crown flame length, ft	Fireline intensity, Btu/ft/s	Crown flame length, m	Fireline intensity, kJ/m/s
20	1000	5	2570
30	1840	10	7280
40	2830	15	13,400
50	3950	20	20,600
75	7260	25	29,800
100	11,200	30	37,800
125	15,600	40	58,200
150	20,500	50	81,400
175	25,900	60	107,000
200	31,600	70	135,000
225	37,700	80	165,000
250	44,200	90	197,000
275	51,000	100	230,000
300	58,100		

Nomograms (or nomographs) are a graphical means of calculating fire behavior. The upper right quadrant of some nomograms is based on the same relationships as the fire characteristics chart. The original nomograms (Albini 1976b) graphed rate of spread versus reaction intensity, with flame length curves. Those nomograms were later reproduced in Rothermel (1983), with the X-axis rescaled to be heat per unit area to facilitate obtaining values to plot on a fire characteristics chart. Rothermel's (1991) crown fire nomograms include a similar plot, with flame length curves also labeled with values for unit power of the fire (which is compared to unit power of the wind). Nomographs developed by Scott (2007) do not produce intermediate values such as heat per unit area, so they do not include a fire characteristics chart graph.

Andrews and Rothermel (1982) provided fire characteristics charts in a form suitable for copying. The fire behavior chart was produced with two scales, one labeled "Scale for Heavy Fuels" with higher heat per unit area and lower rate of spread. Neither version covered the entire range of possible values. To overcome that limitation, they also provided a form of the chart that used logarithmic scales on the axes. They cautioned that "Because a primary purpose of the fire characteristics chart is to visually illustrate changes in fire behavior, care should be taken in interpretation of relative location of points plotted on the logarithmic chart." Given the difficulty in interpreting plotted values using a logarithmic scale and the fact that the program allows the scale to be set to a wide range of possible values, this option is not offered in our program.

The FARSITE program uses a fire characteristics chart to display fire front characteristics during a simulation of fire growth (Finney 1998). For each time step, surface or crown fire rate of spread and heat per unit area are plotted for each pixel. The curves on the chart are labeled with Byram's flame length values regardless of fire type. The changing cloud of points provides a general representation of changes in fire behavior with space and time.

Cruz and others (2008) plotted observed head fire rate of spread and fuel consumed in relation to type of fire (surface or crown) and six levels of Byram's (1959) fireline intensity, assuming a constant heat of combustion. This relationship is based on calculation of fireline intensity from total fuel consumed rather than the fuel consumed in the flaming front.

The Canadian system of fire danger rating has been used to produce "fire intensity class graphs." Head fireline intensity for a Canadian Fire Behavior Prediction (FBP) System fuel type is based on the Initial Spread Index (ISI) and Buildup Index (BUI) components of the Canadian Forest Fire Weather Index (FWI) System (e.g., Alexander and Cole 1995; Cole and Alexander 1995). The relationships require that a separate graph be produced for each FBP System fuel type.

A fire characteristics chart was developed for the U.S. National Fire Danger Rating System (NFDRS) based on the relationship among Spread Component (SC), Energy Release Component (ERC), and Burning Index (BI) (Andrews and Rothermel 1982). BI is a function of SC and ERC, allowing BI curves to be plotted on a chart. The program described in this paper will be expanded to include the option of plotting U.S. NFDRS indices.

5 References

Albini, Frank A. 1976a. Computer-based models of wildland fire behavior: a user's manual. Gen. Tech. Rep. Ogden, UT: U.S. Department of Agriculture, Forest Service, Intermountain Forest and Range Experiment Station. 68 p.

Albini, Frank A. 1976b. Estimating wildfire behavior and effects. Gen. Tech. Rep. INT-30. Ogden, UT: U.S. Department of Agriculture, Forest Service, Intermountain Forest and Range Experiment Station. 92 p.

Alexander, M. E.; Cole, F. V. 1995. Predicting and interpreting fire intensities in Alaskan black spruce forests using the Canadian system of fire danger rating. In: Managing Forests to Meet People's Needs: Proceedings of 1994 Society of American Foresters/Canadian Institute of Forestry Convention; 18-22 September, 1994; Anchorage, Alaska. 95-02. Bethesda, Maryland: Society of American Foresters: 185-192.

Anderson, Hal E. 1968. Sundance fire: an analysis of fire phenomena. Res. Pap. INT-56. Ogden, UT: U.S. Department of Agriculture, Forest Service, Intermountain Forest and Range Experiment Station. 37 p.

Anderson, Hal E. 1969. Heat transfer and fire spread. Res. Pap. INT-69. Ogden, UT: U.S. Department of Agriculture, Forest Service, Intermountain Forest and Range Experiment Station. 20 p.

Anderson, Hal E. 1982. Aids to determining fuel models for estimating fire behavior. Gen. Tech. Rep. INT-122. Ogden, UT: U.S. Department of Agriculture, Forest Service, Intermountain Forest and Range Experiment Station. 22 p.

Andrews, Patricia L. 2007. BehavePlus fire modeling system: past, present, and future. In: Proceedings of 7th Symposium on Fire and Forest Meteorology; 2007 October 23-25; Bar Harbor, Maine: 13.

Andrews, Patricia L.; Bevins, Collin D.; Seli, Robert C. 2008. BehavePlus fire modeling system, version 4.0: User's guide. Gen. Tech. Rep. RMRS-GTR-106WWW [Revised]. Fort Collins, CO: U.S. Department of Agriculture, Forest Service, Rocky Mountain Research Station. 116 p.

Andrews, Patricia L.; Rothermel, Richard C. 1982. Charts for interpreting wildland fire behavior characteristics. Gen. Tech. Rep. INT-131. Ogden, UT: U.S. Department of Agriculture, Forest Service, Intermountain Forest and Range Experiment Station. 21 p.

Brown, A. A.; Davis, K. P. 1973. Fire Effects. In: Forest Fire Control and Use, 2nd Edition. New York, NY: McGraw-Hill Book Co., Inc.: Chap. 3.

Byram, George M. 1959. Combustion of forest fuels. In: Davis, Kenneth P. Forest Fire Control and Use. New York, NY: McGraw-Hill Book Co.: Chap. 3.

USDA Forest Service Gen. Tech. Rep. RMRS-GTR-253. 2011

37

Cole, F. V.; Alexander, M. E. 1995. Head fire intensity class graph for FBP system fuel type C-2 (Boreal Spruce). Alaska Department of Natural Resources, Division of Forestry, Fairbanks, AK, and Canadian Forest Service, Northern Forestry Centre, Edmonton, AB. Poster (with text).

Cruz, Miguel G.; Alexander, Martin E.; Fernandes, Paulo A. M. 2008. Development of a model system to predict wildfire behaviour in pine plantations. Australian Forestry. 71(2): 113-121.

Finney, Mark A. 1998. FARSITE: Fire Area Simulator-model development and evaluation. Res. Pap. RMRS-RP-4. Ogden, UT: U.S. Department of Agriculture, Forest Service, Rocky Mountain Research Station. 47 p.

Hodgson, Athol. 1968. Control burning in eucalypt forests in Victoria, Australia. Journal of Forestry. 66(8): 601-605.

Hough, W. A. 1968. Fuel consumption and fire behavior of hazard reduction burns. Res. Pap. SE-36. Asheville, NC: U.S. Department of Agriculture, Forest Service, Southeastern Forest Experiment Station. 7 p.

Kiil, A. D. 1975. Fire spread in a black spruce stand. Canadian Forest Service Bi-Monthly Research Notes. 31(1): 2-3.

Kilgore, Bruce M.; Sando, Rodney W. 1975. Crown-fire potential in a sequoia forest after prescribed burning. Forest Science. 21(1): 83-87.

Mann, Jim. 1974. [Personal Communication]. U.S. Department of Agriculture, Forest Service, Region 3.

McArthur, A. G. 1967. Fire behaviour in Eucalypt forests. Leaflet 107. Canberra, Australia: Commonwealth of Australia, Department of National Development, Forest and Timber Bureau, Canberra. 36 p.

Methven, Ian R.; Murray, W. G. 1974. Using fire to eliminate understory balsam fir in pine management. The Forestry Chronicle. 50(2): 1-3.

National Fire Protection Association. 1990. Black Tiger Fire: Case study of the wildland/urban interface fire that destroyed 44 homes and other structures near Boulder, Colorado, July 9, 1989. Quincy, MA: Fire Investigations Division, National Fire Protection Association. 40 p.

Rothermel, Richard C. 1972. A mathematical model for predicting fire spread in wildland fuels. Res. Pap. INT-115. Ogden, UT: U.S. Department of Agriculture, Forest Service, Intermountain Forest and Range Experiment Station. 40 p.

Rothermel, Richard C. 1983. How to predict the spread and intensity of forest and range fires. Gen. Tech. Rep. INT-143. Ogden, UT: U.S. Department of Agriculture, Forest Service, Intermountain Forest and Range Experiment Station. 161 p.

Rothermel, Richard C. 1984. Fire behavior consideration of aerial ignition. Workshop: Prescribed Fire by Aerial Ignition. Intermountain Fire Council, Missoula, MT: 143-158.

Rothermel, Richard C. 1991. Predicting behavior and size of crown fires in the northern Rocky Mountains. Res. Pap. INT-438. Ogden, UT: U.S. Department of Agriculture, Forest Service, Intermountain Research Station. 46 p.

Rothermel, Richard C. 2009. Use a crayon to model fire behavior. Learning from the experts. Wildland Fire Lessons Learned Center, Tucson, Arizona. Available: http://MyFireVideos.net.

Rothermel, Richard C.; Anderson, Hal E. 1966. Fire spread characteristics determined in the laboratory. Res. Pap. INT-30. Ogden, UT: U.S. Department of Agriculture, Forest Service, Intermountain Forest and Range Experiment Station. 34 p.

Rothermel, Richard C.; Deeming, John E. 1980. Measuring and interpreting fire behavior for correlation with fire effects. Gen. Tech. Rep. INT-93. Ogden, UT: U.S. Department of Agriculture, Forest Service, Intermountain Forest and Range Experiment Station. 4 p.

Roussopoulos, Peter J. 1974. Fire intensity levels. National Fuel Management Workshop. 3 p.

Scott, Joe H. 2007. Nomographs for estimating surface fire behavior characteristics. Gen. Tech. Rep. RMRS-GTR-192. Fort Collins, CO: U.S. Department of Agriculture, Forest Service, Rocky Mountain Research Station. 119 p.

Scott, Joe H.; Burgan, Robert E. 2005. Standard fire behavior fuel models: a comprehensive set for use with Rothermel's surface fire spread model. RMRS-GTR-153. Fort Collins, CO: U.S. Department of Agriculture, Forest Service, Rocky Mountain Research Station. 72 p.

Thomas, P. H. 1963. The size of flames from natural fires. In: Proceedings, 9th International Symposium on Combustion; 1962; Ithaca, NY: Academic Press: 844-859.

U.S. Department of Agriculture [USDA]; U.S. Department of the Interior [USDOI]. 2008. Interagency prescribed fire: planning and implementation procedure guide. Boise, ID: National Wildfire Coordinating Group. 50 p.

Van Wagner, C. E. 1968. Fire behavior mechanisms in a red pine plantation: field and laboratory evidence. Departmental Publication. No. 1229. Ottawa, Ontario, Canada: Canada Department of Forestry and Rural Development, Forestry Branch. 30 p.

Van Wagner, C. E. 1975. Conditions and criteria for the spread of crown fire. Draft. Unpublished copy, Canadian Forestry Service, Petawawa Forest Experiment Station. 20 p.

Walker, J. D.; Stocks, B. J. 1972. Analysis of two 1971 wildfires in Ontario: Thackeray and Whistle Lake. Inf. Rep. O-X-166. Sault Ste. Marie, Ontario, Canada: Department of the Environment, Canadian Forestry Service, Great Lakes Research Centre. 13 p.

Appendix A. Fire Intensity Levels _____

Fire Intensity Levels

Initial Summary used at National Fuel Management Workshop (Roussopoulos 1974).*

Fireline intensity (*Btu/ft/s*)	Calculated flame length (*ft*)	Fire descriptions and control actions
Level I:		
2-3	<1	Few fires exist at this low intensity. (Byram 1959)
Level II:		
19-58	2-3	Most prescribed fires are backing into the wind in surface fuels. The depth of the flaming zone is less than 1 foot and the flame length is about 2 feet. (Brown and Davis 1973)
20-100	2-4	Prescribed backfires in slash-longleaf pine with palmetto-gallberry understory reduced surface fuels and did little damage to the overstory. Higher intensities resulted in stand damage, especially with low winds; rates of spread between 1.5 and 3 ft/min. (Hough 1968)
24	2	A test fire in a balsam fir understory with a tree height of 13 feet and a crown base height of 3 feet. The crown bulk density was moderate to light at 0.0087 lb/ft^3. The fire would not sustain crowning, only occasional torching. The surface fire is below the critical level. (Methven and Murray 1974)
27	2	The fire was in the surface fuels of a eucalypt forest with a fuel load of 3.4 tons/acre of fuels less than $\frac{1}{4}$ inch in diameter. The surface rate of spread is about 1.1 ft/min, and the flame length was about 12-15 inches. (McArthur 1967)
100	4	In eucalypt forests, this level of intensity generally represents the limit of control for manual ground attack. Flame lengths exceed 3 feet and the surface rate of spread is about 4 ft/min. This is the maximum prescribed intensity for controlled burning activities. (Hodgson 1968)
Level III:		
100-1000	4-11	Prescribed and wildfires are burning with the wind in surface fuels. Most fires are controlled by direct attack with conventional firefighting methods and are considered to be two-dimensional fires. At the upper end of the range, flame lengths will be about 9 feet and heat from fire will be intense at a distance of 30-40 feet from fire. (Brown and Davis 1973)
112	4	Fire was in the surface fuels of a eucalypt forest. The fuel load was 6.5 tons/acre fuels for fuels less than ¼ inch in diameter. The surface rate of spread was 2.4 ft/min. Flame lengths were as much as 5 feet but averaged 3-4 feet. (McArthur 1967)
210	5	This was a prescribed fire under a three-storied sequoia-mixed conifer stand: white fir saplings (10-50 feet), ponderosa pine/incense cedar (100-180 feet), and sequoia (180-250 feet). The rate of spread was about 7.5 ft/min with a combustion rate of 6367 Btu/min/ft^2. The live crown base changed from 3 feet to 16 feet, and the live crown load was reduced from 7.2 to 3.1 tons/acre. (Kilgore and Sando 1975)
500	8	This fireline intensity represents the upper limit for good control. Serious spotting limits attack. In a eucalypt forest, flame heights reach 8 feet. (Hodgson 1968)

USDA Forest Service Gen. Tech. Rep. RMRS-GTR-253. 2011

39

Fireline intensity (*Btu/ft/s*)	Calculated flame length (*ft*)	Fire descriptions and control actions
Level III:		
700	9	This intensity represents the limit for fires in ponderosa pine stands of Region 3 (U.S. Forest Service) that can be contained by initial attack forces. It was used to set slash residue limits. (Mann 1974, personal communication)
725	9 surface 23 crowning	These test fires were monitored in a red pine plantation with a tree height of 46 feet and a crown base height of 23 feet. Crown bulk density was moderate at 0.0162 lb/ft^3. Crowning occurred for up to 2 minutes with flame lengths 20-23 feet above the crown. The crown fire was dependent upon the surface fire. (Van Wagner 1968)
Level IV:		
>1000	11	This represents the intensity above which spotting, torching, and crowning activities contribute significantly to fire spread and resistance to suppression.
1209	12	This test fire was in a Canadian black spruce stand 14 feet high with a total load of about 15 tons/acre. About 54% of the crowns were burned, mainly by torching of clumps. Spotting was experienced up to 200 feet ahead of the front in a wind of 12 mi/h. (Kiil 1975)
1148-1390	11-13	This intensity was experienced in a test fire in a jack pine stand 66 feet high with crown base of 39 feet. Crown bulk density was light at 0.0062 lb/ft^3. No crowning occurred. (Van Wagner 1975)
2900	18	In a stand with about 50% crown closure, fire achieved crowning but was dependent on ground fire. (Van Wagner 1975)
2000-6500	15-26	Crown fires in standing pine were observed with rates of spread from 35 to 90 ft/min. Flame lengths were observed to be 49-69 feet, exceeding about 26 feet above the tree canopy. (Van Wagner 1968)
10,500	32	These conditions were found at the 1971 Thackary Fire in Ontario. (Walker and Stocks 1972)
13,500	36	These conditions were found at the 1971 Whistle Lake Fire in Ontario. (Walker and Stocks 1972)
22,500	45	Extensive crowning, long-range spotting, tree breakage and blowdown all occurred during high-intensity portions of the 1967 Sundance Fire. (Anderson 1968)
30,000	52	This level of intensity represents a major fast-spreading fire with flame depth to 0-0.25 mile or more and flame heights from 50 to 150 feet. A change in fuels and/or weather is needed to suppress such a fire. (Brown and Davis 1973)

*Minor editorial changes have been made to the original text.